Speech and Language Services and the Classroom Teacher

Gerald G. Freeman
Oakland Schools
Pontiac, Michigan

A publication of the National Support Systems Project under a grant from the Division of Personnel Preparation, Bureau of Education for the Handicapped, U.S. Office of Education, Department of Health, Education, and Welfare.

This project was performed pursuant to Grant No. 600-75-0913 from the Division of Personnel Preparation, Bureau of Education for the Handicapped, U.S. Office of Education, Department of Health, Education, and Welfare. The printing of this publication was supported in part by Grant No. OEG-0-9-336005-2452 from the Exceptional Children's Program, Bureau of Adult and Occupational Education, U. S. Office of Education, Department of Health, Education, and Welfare. The point of view expressed herein is the author's and does not necessarily reflect the position or policy of the U.S. Office of Education, and no official endorsement by the U. S. Office of Education should be inferred.

Minneapolis, Minnesota
1977

Copies may be ordered from The Council for Exceptional Children, 1920 Association Drive, Reston, Virginia 22091. Contact CEC Publications Sales Unit for current single copy price and for quantity order discount rates.

ACKNOWLEDGEMENTS

More than 70 interviews were held with classroom teachers, speech-language pathologists, and school administrators in the course of preparing this book. I am grateful to all of them for taking the time to share their experiences and observations with me. Those who were especially helpful are as follows:

Mrs. Anne G. Cann
Coordinator of Language and Speech Services
Amherst-Pelham Regional Schools
Amherst, Massachusetts

Dr. Robert L. Huskey
Assistant Superintendent
Department of Speech and Hearing
Special School District of Saint Louis County
Town and Country, Missouri

Mrs. Patricia Kaelber
Project Director
Project Right to Achieve
Gouldsboro Grammar School
Gouldsboro, Maine

Mr. Arthur Kelley
Supervisor of Language Classes
Special School District of Saint Louis County
Town and Country, Missouri

Dr. Harold J. McGrady
Director of Special Education
Mesa Public Schools
Mesa, Arizona

Mrs. Kathleen Pendergast
Supervisor of Language, Speech and Hearing
Seattle Public Schools
Seattle, Washington

Mrs. Marisue Pickering
Lecturer and Staff Speech Pathologist
Department of Speech Communication
University of Maine
Orono, Maine

Mrs. Sally Randall
Speech Pathologist
Greensboro City Schools
Greensboro, North Carolina

Mr. Frank Saunders
Director of Exceptional Child Services
Greensboro City Schools
Greensboro, North Carolina

Ms. Jo Ann Schall
Speech and Language Specialist
Mesa Public Schools
Mesa, Arizona

iv

I would like to thank the National Support Systems Project for making this project possible. I am particularly indebted to Dr. Maynard Reynolds, Director, Karen Lundholm, Assistant to the Director, and Sylvia W. Rosen, editor, for their encouragement, support, and assistance.

This project could not have been completed without the constructive and invaluable suggestions of Ruth H. Freeman. Also, I wish to acknowledge the administration and staff of the Oakland Schools whose pride in their members' accomplishments provides limitless motivation.

Finally, special mention must be made of Mrs. Juanita Garner, Mrs. Ruth Smith, Mrs. Marilyn Lund, and Kathy Bass (of the NSSP staff) for their help in typing the manuscript.

G. G. F.

FOREWORD

As school systems face up to the task of programing children with special needs according to the least restrictive alternative, changes in the roles of both regular and special education personnel necessarily ensue. Instead of maintaining separate domains of operations, special and regular educators must work together and share the necessary skills, methods, and materials to provide special services for the children with special needs mostly within the regular classroom. In this endeavor, a wide array of specialists is essential to provide classroom teachers with total support.

In this book, Dr. Freeman demonstrates that special speech and language services can be provided in the regular classroom through the collaborative efforts of speech-language pathologists and regular classroom teachers. In doing so, he describes six programs which he observed in operation in different school systems around the country, and he analyzes not only how the programs work but, also, why they work successfully.

In the opening chapters, Dr. Freeman presents a brief primer on the speech and language problems which may be encountered among children in regular education classrooms. These materials epitomize the kind of sharing which, he believes, should characterize the specialist-regular teacher relationship. The second part of the book contains the descriptions of the programs.

Dr. Freeman (his Ph.D. is from the University of Michigan) is eminently qualified to address the problems of providing speech and language services to children in regular education classrooms. He has been the Director of the Oakland Schools Speech and Hearing Clinic for 19 years and he is a consultant to the speech and language programs in the 28 constituent districts of the Oakland Schools. Dr. Freeman is a Fellow of the American Speech and Hearing Association in which he has served on numerous committees and as Vice-President for Clinical Affairs. He has been a visiting faculty member at eight universities and is the author of several articles and chapters of books on the management of children with speech and language problems. Further, he is the editor of the journal, *Language, Speech and Hearing Services in Schools.*

The development of this publication is one of the activities of the National Support Systems (NSS) Project enabled by the Bureau of Education for the Handicapped, Division of Personnel Preparation. Initially authorized under the Education Professions Development Act as the Leadership Training Institute/Special Education, the project has focused primarily on the training of regular education teachers to increase their ability to accommodate children with handicaps in their classrooms and on the support of special education teachers to increase their skills to work with regular education teachers. The literature resulting from these activities ranges from descriptive materials on mainstreaming children with specific handicaps to presentations of specific skills and techniques. In the program of NSS-LTI publications, Freeman's book belongs with four others that describe emerging mainstreaming practices:

vi

Jack W. Birch, *Mainstreaming: Educable mentally retarded children in regular classes.*

Jack W. Birch, *Hearing impaired children in the mainstream.*

Glenda Martin & Mollie Hoben, *Supporting visually impaired students in the mainstream.*

Evelyn N. Deno, *Mainstreaming: Learning disabled, emotionally disturbed, and socially maladjusted children in regular classes.* (Winter 1977)

A complete listing of the publications is given at the end of this book.

Since the pupil population of concern in this book usually is found in regular classrooms, Dr. Freeman's presentation centers less on the administrative problems of mainstreaming and more on the actual delivery of needed special services. Hence, the programs described lend themselves to generalization and offer suggestions for the delivery of many other kinds of special services in regular classrooms through the cooperation of specialists and regular teachers.

Maynard C. Reynolds, Director
National Support Systems Project
University of Minnesota

CONTENTS

PREFACE

This book is based on the premise that successful speech and language services in the schools must include the participation of classroom teachers. It is intended to enable elementary classroom teachers to broaden their understanding of speech and language development and its disorders, and to develop insight into the field of speech and language pathology. The book highlights the importance of teachers in meeting the auditory-verbal needs of all children and, in particular, those with communicative problems.

Although the concept of interdisciplinary cooperation between teachers and speech-language specialists is not new, frequently, these professionals have failed to interact effectively to achieve their common goals. On the one hand, some teachers have been satisfied to delegate the total responsibility for children's verbal communicative needs to speech-language specialists. These teachers have viewed auditory-verbal skills as circumscribed behaviors that have little to do with academic achievement. On the other hand, some school speech-language specialists have failed to establish that their roles and functions are significant, even essential, to the academic program. They have conducted their services surrounded by an aura of specialization.

Current educational philosophy has emphasized the importance of varied interdisciplinary school programs to meet the different individual needs of children. However, the success of such programs is largely dependent upon the ability of the participating professionals to establish compatible working relations. These professionals, aside from their own areas of expertise and competence, must share a common body of knowledge and concepts. They must appreciate each other's professional capabilities and limitations so that they may complement and supplement each other's efforts.

1

The material in this book may be used by classroom teachers and school speech-language specialists as a step in this direction. The book does not purport to train classroom teachers to become speech-language specialists. Rather, it shares information, as one professional to another, about the nature and implications of school speech and language services. As a result of reading the book, it is hoped that teachers and speech-language specialists will be better able to assess each other's unique and overlapping professional contributions. If so, perhaps they will use the book as a catalyst for establishing or improving the close working relations that are necessary to achieve the educational goals common to both professions.

G. G. F.

I

INTRODUCTION

Elementary classroom teachers are being called upon to become more and more active in the management of children with verbal communicative problems. This situation has developed because (a) educators are placing greater emphasis on the relation between verbal communicative skills and reading, (b) more children with special education needs, including speech and language, are being placed in regular classrooms, and (c) changes are occurring in the concept and implementation of school-based remedial speech and language programs. All of these factors demand the greater involvement of classroom teachers in meeting the auditory-verbal needs of children.

Auditory-Verbal Skills and Reading

Language arts programs have long recognized that verbal comprehension, oral expression, reading, and writing are progressive linguistic skills. Yet, early elementary curricula often place immediate emphasis on teaching reading, overlooking the fact that some children have failed to master verbal comprehension and oral expression before entering school. Similarly, if children have difficulties in comprehending spoken language or in speaking, reading, or writing, their problems tend to be viewed as circumscribed and independently remediable rather than interrelated. The responsibility for the management of breakdowns in any linguistic mode, therefore, is delegated to a specialist—speech or reading—depending upon the predominant symptom.

Currently, school personnel recognize that the development of auditory-verbal skills significantly relates to children's achievements in other language modes. In fact, the primary language skills are prerequisite to literacy; reading is dependent on language (Kavanaugh, 1968; Venezky, 1968). The development of auditory-verbal skills, therefore, assumes a prominence in the curriculum that clearly places it within the responsibilities of classroom teachers as well as of speech and language specialists and reading experts, and requires the coordination of their various competencies.

Mainstreaming

The changes in educational policy resulting from recent adjudications and legislation have led to the greater inclusion of children with special needs in regular classrooms. This process, frequently called "mainstreaming," is intended to provide handicapped children with as many normal educational, social, and personal experiences as possible. It establishes regular classrooms as the base for the educational programing of handicapped children, even though they may need supplementary special education and resource services. In mainstreaming, classroom teachers coordinate the programs necessary to achieve the children's individual educational objectives.

Most elementary teachers are accustomed to the presence of children with verbal communicative differences in their classes. Some of these children have *speech* disorders, that is, they mispronounce words, stutter, or have unusual voice qualities. Others have *language* problems, that is, they have mild to moderate difficulty recalling words, formulating and expressing sentences, and understanding speech. Although most such children attend speech classes for the remediation of their verbal communicative differences, they generally are able to participate in the regular academic program.

Speech and language specialists have relied on teachers to (a) refer children with suspected verbal communi-

4

cative problems, (b) participate in evaluative procedures by providing historical and observational information, and (c) promote the integration of children's newly acquired communicative skills into daily classroom activities. In such remedial programs, teachers have been involved only peripherally. In mainstreaming, in contrast, classroom teachers are placed in a central role of planning and implementing programs for the development of verbal skills. Because the incidence of auditory-verbal problems is high among all categories of educationally impaired children and the development of primary language skills is basic to their academic achievement, teachers must assume a major role in meeting the needs of these children. In short, teachers, the central figures in regular education, are also becoming central figures in special education, including speech and language programs.

Changes in Remedial Speech and Language Programs

For more than 50 years, school districts have employed specialists to help children with auditory-verbal problems. These professionals have been known variously as speech teachers, speech correctionists, teachers of the speech impaired, speech clinicians, speech specialists, speech consultants, and speech pathologists. To emphasize their contributions to language development and its disorders, some of these professionals have changed their titles to "speech-language teachers," "teachers of the speech and language impaired," and the like. The American Speech and Hearing Association (ASHA), in 1977, designated "speech-language pathologist" as the official professional title of qualified individuals who provide services to persons with verbal communicative disorders (Report of the Legislative Council, 1977).

It has been the responsibility of the professionals now known as school speech-language pathologists to evaluate children, diagnose their verbal communicative problems, if any, and formulate and direct plans that facilitate improvement in their skills. For many years, the speech-language pathologists fulfilled these responsibilities by conducting itinerant programs in which they traveled from school to school to work with small groups of children on a biweekly basis. In 1974, however, ASHA stated that a comprehensive school speech and language program should provide a *continuum* of services (Healey, 1974). This continuum recognizes the wide range of needs among children and accommodates each. It is marked by three key points or components: (a) communicative development on one extreme, (b) communicative deviations in the center, and (c) communicative disorders on the other extreme.

The school speech-language pathologist who is committed to delivering services along this continuum recognizes the need for (a) insuring communicative competence for all children, (b) providing direct or indirect service to children who demonstrate mild or transitory deviations, and (c) working intensively with children whose communicative disorders interfere with academic achievement and/or social adjustment. This concept of service covers a span of functions from the prevention of speech and language problems to the remediation or alleviation of serious communicative disorders.

In order to accomplish these goals, the school speech-language pathologist must use a variety of service and scheduling models. The well-established itinerant model does not provide the flexibility and diversification necessary to meet the range of children's needs. In addition, the speech-language pathologist must involve classroom teachers variously at different points along the continuum. In the case of preventive services, for example, teacher consultations with or without classroom demonstrations by the speech-language pathologist may be most appropriate. At the other extreme, services to children with serious language disorders may consist of placement in a transitional class, resource room, or regular classroom with intensive supportive services from the speech-language pathologist. In all instances, classroom teachers are an integral part of the identification, evaluation, and management procedures.

For these reasons it is important for classroom teachers to understand verbal communication and its disorders, the field of speech and language pathology, and the ways in which interdisciplinary cooperation promotes the development of auditory-verbal skills along the continuum of elementary school children's needs.

Organization of Presentation

The book is divided into two parts. Part 1 consists of, first, an overview of verbal communication and its disorders and, second, a description of school speech and language services. The material on the major types of verbal communicative problems—articulation, voice, fluency, and language—is a review for teachers who are knowledgeable in speech and language pathology and an introduction for those who have limited background or experience in this area.

The discussion of the major components of a school speech and language program—identification, evaluation, and remediation—should be of equal value to all teachers. It is intended to acquaint teachers with the roles and responsibilities of speech-language pathologists and the relations of these functions to education. It emphasizes the need for interdisciplinary cooperation in areas of overlapping concern and the ways in which teachers are essential to the success of various aspects of school speech and language services.

Part 2 mainly consists of descriptions of six programs that exemplify successful cooperative efforts between classroom teachers and speech-language pathologists in the delivery of speech and language services. The programs demonstrate the types of improved services that can develop when classroom teachers and speech-language pathologists share an understanding of verbal communication and its disorders, the relation of speech-language services to educational goals, and the potential of teachers to facilitate improved verbal skills.

All the programs described were observed by the author. Each is a model for one of the three critical points along the speech-language service continuum—early intervention-prevention, speech deviations, and communicative disorders. The districts in which the programs are operating vary in location, size, and administrative arrangement, thus demonstrating the range of adaptations that is possible.

The descriptions of the programs dynamically relate the didactic materials of Chapters II and III to real-life situations. They offer teachers, speech-language pathologists, and administrators practical suggestions on how to expand and improve their own programs through the greater involvement of classroom teachers.

PART 1

II

VERBAL COMMUNICATION AND ITS DISORDERS

Children learn to understand and speak the languages of their cultures; in fact, by 3 years of age most children are able to engage in fairly sophisticated conversation. They appropriately produce a sufficient number of the sounds of their native languages to be understood. They comprehend the sentences of other people and put words together into meaningful sentences. They have internalized the linguistic rules for meanings of words and word combinations, as well as for ordering words into various sentence types. Considering the complexities involved in mastering these skills, it is amazing that most children accomplish the task at all, let alone in so brief a time.

Speech and language are generically the same; that is, speech is vocal language. However, it is convenient to separate the two in order to study and understand verbal communication and its disorders. For these purposes, *language* is considered to be a set of symbols that represent a conceptual system used by man to communicate. This linguistic code may be expressed orally in speech or graphically in writing (Carrow, 1972). *Speech* is the oral expression of symbols, the motor act of transmitting symbols to another person by converting them to acoustic signals via movements of the articulators and vocal tract (Cooper, 1972).

In order to develop speech and language, children must be able to produce sounds, recognize their symbolic features, and learn that given sequences of sound have meaning. These skills require physical integrity. They also depend upon people, objects, and events in the environment.

Physical Requisites for Speech

The processes involved in human sound production are respiration, phonation, resonation, and articulation. Respiration, or breathing, provides the source of energy for sound production. The breathstream activates the vocal cords, causing them to vibrate and produce sound, or to phonate. This sound is then transmitted to the cavities and bones of the head and neck where it is resonated— conserved and concentrated—to give a characteristic quality to each voice. Finally, through movements of the parts of the mouth, the sound is shaped into the phonemes of language and articulated with other sounds as speech.

A breakdown in one or more of these systems interferes with speech sound production. For example, children who are unable to control the breathstream because of neuromuscular difficulties are unable to sustain a tone long enough to support the production of successive phonemes. Or, if their breathing mechanisms are intact but their vocal cords lack enervation (phonatory breakdown), they may produce limited tones or none at all. Indeed, any abnormal condition of the vocal cords, such as inflammation, nodes, or thickening, is likely to interfere with clear voice quality.

The most common resonance disturbances involve nasality. All but three English sounds, *m, n,* and *ng,* are resonated predominantly in the mouth; *m, n,* and *ng* are nasally resonated. If a cleft in the roof of the mouth or other physical condition leads to excessive nasal resonance, the speaker's voice quality is hypernasal. Under these conditions, an utterance such as "buy baby a bib" sounds like "my mamy a mim." However, when the nasal cavity is blocked and *m, n,* and *ng* are produced predominantly through the mouth, a denasal or hyponasal voice quality results, as in the well-known phrase, "sprig has cub."

Finally, children who are unable to move the articulators—tongue, lips, and jaws—or coordinate articulatory movements may have trouble producing individual sounds or making rapid transitions from one phoneme to another. These problems may interfere with the articulation of a number of sounds, reducing speech intelligibility and communicative effectiveness.

Individual Requisites for Language

Assuming that children are capable sound producers, it is still necesary for them to learn to use the sounds symbolically as language. For this ability, sensory intactness, intelligence, and neurological integrity are among the most significant considerations.

The close and important relation between the sense of hearing and language acquisition is well known. It stands to reason that children must be able to hear a language in order to learn it naturally. The fact that deaf individuals rarely learn spoken language without special measures is testimony to aural-oral dependency. However, young children also receive information about their environment through other senses—taste, smell, touch, and vision. They explore their surroundings and receive information about the physical attributes of the objects there. This input eventually serves as the referential basis for concepts and language. For example, children rarely respond to the word "hot" until a first-hand experience substantiates the sensation represented by the word. They learn "sour" by contrasting tastes, "soft" by contrasting textures, and other descriptors in the same way. Sensory deprivation of any type, therefore, may interfere with language learning.

One aspect of the learning and developmental problems of children with limited intelligence is the inclination to have difficulty mastering language. The language of such children is frequently delayed at a level commensurate with their skills in other areas, develops unevenly, or follows the anticipated sequence of language acquisition but later than the norm.

The relations between neurological integrity and speech and language are numerous and complex. These relations underlie all aspects of the communication chain—verbal reception, integration, and expression. In addition, the nervous system monitors, coordinates, and energizes the structures involved in these processes. In practical terms, neurological problems that involve the ear interfere with children's ability to hear verbal stimuli; central neurological deficits may affect their ability to interpret these stimuli and/or to formulate verbal responses; and inadequate motor coordination may prevent children from making the necessary vocal and articulatory movements for language expression.

Environmental Requisites

Experiences with people and objects are basic to speech and language development. (a) People in the environment tend to surround young children with verbal behavior. Parents, grandparents, siblings, and friends not only serve as linguistic models but also stimulate, motivate, and encourage young children to talk. They reinforce and reward the children's appropriate verbal behavior with hugs, attention, other signs of approval, and additional verbal stimulation. (b) The environment provides children with experiences. Initially, it offers them an endless array of objects to explore, conceptualize, and label. Later, it provides them with opportunities to engage in actions and events that are worth discussing. Breakdowns in environmental circumstances may interfere with speech and language development. For example, excessive speech demands or stimulation beyond children's capabilities may discourage rather than encourage verbal interchange. In addition, the environment that provides limited possibilities for exploration and exposure to varying events tends to restrict the experiential background necessary for concept and language development.

In sum, the development of speech and language is complex. It requires the integration of children's physical attributes and their environmental circumstances. Although the two entities have been separated for purposes of discussion, in everyday life they frequently are inextricable. Speech and language behavior at once reflects and inflects environments, and vice versa.

Speech and Language Problems

Verbal communicative problems are usually classified into four broad categories: (a) articulation, (b) voice, (c) fluency, and (d) language. Within each category the severity of problems ranges from barely noticeable, relatively nontroublesome deviations, to severe communicative disorders that interfere with academic achievement, self-esteem, and social adjustment. Children in any elementary classroom are likely to demonstrate a full range of verbal skills, from clear, effective speech and language to complicated communicative disorders. Therefore, it is important that teachers understand the nature of speech and language problems.

13

ARTICULATORY PROBLEMS

Articulatory problems consist of substitutions, omissions, and distortions of consonant and/or vowel sounds. These errors are not mutually exclusive. Frequently, they all occur in the speech patterns of children with communicative disorders. Children who demonstrate a number of phonemic errors, like those that follow, are said to have "multiple articulatory problems":

Typical sound substitutions include w/r ("wun"/run), f/th ("fumb"/thumb), and d/g ("gog"/dog). The substitution of th/s ("theven"/seven) that is so common among elementary children is called an *interdental lisp*.

Examples of omissions are: "no"/nose (z), "pay"/play (l), "tep"/step (s).

Distortions are substitutions of non-English sounds for English phonemes. They often occur when a child directs the airstream out of one or both sides of the mouth, instead of centrally, during the production of sibilant sounds (s, z, sh, zh, ch, j). The resulting phonemes are "slushy." Since the airstream is directed laterally, the problem is called a *lateral lisp.*

Most children demonstrate a number of developmental or maturational articulatory errors as they learn to use correct speech sounds consistently. Since the normal range of the development of articulation extends to 7 or 8 years of age (Arlt & Goodban, 1976; Templin, 1957), some of these errors are likely to persist until then. Among the most common maturational errors are the substitution of w/l and r, f/th, th/s, and d/g, as well as the omission of final consonant sounds in words and phonemes in blend combinations.

In the past, before our current knowledge and experience were available, school speech-language pathologists worked directly with large numbers of children whose articulatory deviations were actually developmental and who might have progressed satisfactorily without intervention. Believing that the deviations were well-established habits, the speech-language pathologists were able to take credit for modifying deviant speech patterns that could have modified themselves. Today, the range of normal articulatory development is well known; more appropriate procedures of caseload selection have been developed (Zemmol, 1977); and only children whose articulatory problems are bona fide communicative disorders are recognized as needing direct intervention.

Early elementary-school-age children who demonstrate maturational articulatory errors, however, stand to benefit from the indirect speech improvement techniques that may be used by teachers. The techniques include (a) immediate correct repetition of utterances, emphasizing the phonemes in error without demanding modification of the deviations, (b) praising clear speech, and (c) accepting maturational articulatory errors as normal.

VOICE PROBLEMS

The major determinants of an adequate voice are pitch, quality, loudness, and inflection. Deviations in these vocal dimensions, such as hoarseness or a falsetto or too soft a voice, frequently are symptomatic of underlying physical abnormalities and/or vocal misuse or abuse. Therefore, school speech-language pathologists are careful to refer children with voice problems to medical specialists, usually otolaryngologists, for evaluation and possible treatment prior to instituting remedial voice improvement programs.

Vocal pitch is judged according to age and sex. Although postpubescent pitch is differentiated by the sex of the speaker, the pitch ranges of young children are fairly uniform. Occasionally, an elementary-school-age child demonstrates an unusually low- or high-pitched voice that calls undue attention to itself, interferes with communication, and demands remediation.

Deviations in voice quality are more common. They include vocal differences that (a) result from inadequate laryngeal or vocal cord functions and (b) are related to resonance disturbances. For example, hoarseness, harshness, stridency, lack of voice, and breathiness (whisper superimposed on tone) are all indicative of inappropriate vocal cord function. Remedial programs for these disorders are geared to reducing vocal abuse and establishing efficient vocal habit patterns. On the other hand, hypernasality (too nasal) and hyponasality (denasal), as illustrated in a preceding section, are resonance problems. Children who demonstrate these difficulties must learn to redistribute their vocal output between the oral and nasal cavities in order to achieve an appropriate and pleasant resonatory balance.

Speakers moderate their loudness level to accommodate to the situation. However, there usually is at least one child in every classroom whose consistent failure to speak up is the bane of the teacher's existence. Occasionally, these children are physiologically incapable of sustaining adequate breath support, using efficient vocalization, or projecting their voices. They require special services. In most cases, however, a weak, timid voice reflects a child's personality or characteristic adjustment pattern. Withdrawn, fearful, insecure children tend to speak too softly. They need increased confidence, feelings of self-

15

worth, and successful speaking experiences, all of which teachers can help to provide.

Variation in inflection not only adds color to speech but also carries meaning. For example, preschool and kindergarten children sometimes form questions by using declarative statements with a rising inflection, as in "I go home?" "You have a dog?" More sophisticated speakers use emphasis and stress to express humor and sarcasm. Children who do not vary vocal inflection sound monotonous. When accompanied by slow, labored articulation, monotony is sometimes secondary to poor coordination of the vocal and articulatory muscles.

FLUENCY PROBLEMS

Fluency relates to the uninterrupted rate and rhythm, or flow, of speech. All speakers demonstrate occasional inappropriate pauses, vocal interjections ("uh," "well, uh"), and vocal repetitions, but these relatively infrequent dysfluencies do not usually interfere with communication. Individuals who stutter, however, cannot maintain the flow of conversation and demonstrate frequent distracting and troublesome interruptions in the rhythm of speech.

More has been written, yet less is known, about stuttering than any other speech disorder. Symptomatically, stuttering is characterized by speech blocks or interruptions, such as hesitations, repetitions, and prolongations of sounds, words, or phrases. In order to maintain a semblance of fluency, most stutterers also develop a number of additional vocal or nonvocal traits. These secondary symptoms become automatic and an integral part of the primary speech interruptions. For example, when ordering a flavor of ice cream a stutterer may say "Ch-ch-ch-ch-ch" and not be able to finish the word. In order to break the block he/she may try leg tapping, eye blinking, or head jerking, for example, and eventually blurt out "Ch-chocolate." Repeated episodes of this nature lead to the incorporation of the extraneous behaviors with speech. Stuttering, therefore, often involves vocal blocks as well as the secondary mechanisms intended to release them.

Stutterers also are inclined to avoid words and situations that are likely to precipitate their dysfluencies. They become experts in substituting words or avoiding verbal responses by feigning ignorance. At times, they completely stay out of situations in which they feel they will have difficulty speaking.

A number of causes of stuttering have been theorized. Some experts believe it is symptomatic of underlying physical, psychological, or personality problems; others feel it is learned and results from the speaker's simultaneous desire to say something yet avoid dysfluencies; and still others postulate that adults' negative reactions to children's normal speech interruptions elicit anxiety, increased tension, and speech conflicts that lead to stuttering.

In working with stutterers, many school speech-language pathologists combine a symptom-modification program with supportive counseling. This approach is intended to increase fluency while enabling stutterers to gain more insight into their feelings and attitudes about their speech. Classroom teachers may help stutterers by (a) talking with them about their feelings regarding oral recitation; (b) calling on them to recite when they volunteer, rather than surprising them; (c) maintaining eye contact while the children are speaking; (d) calling on them when there is ample time to wait for their responses, not when the bell is about to ring; and (e) removing the emotional charge in speaking situations by providing a well-modulated, easy speech model.

LANGUAGE PROBLEMS

Children with language problems have difficulty in processing sounds, words, and connected speech. They may have trouble *decoding* (i.e., comprehending or interpreting language) or *encoding* (formulating and expressing meaningful utterances). These process disturbances involve one or several of the components of language: phonemes (sounds), semantics (meanings), and syntax (structural relations).

17

The inability to distinguish clearly among sounds is a typical phonological decoding problem. Despite normal hearing acuity, some children have trouble perceiving the differences between similar acoustic signals. For example, when asked, "What melts?" they are likely to respond, "Cows," confusing *melts* with *milks.* Similarly, they may say that garbage *stings,* confusing *stings* with *stinks.* Obviously, these phonological confusions have important semantic overtones. Misarticulations are phonological encoding problems. They, too, may substantially affect or alter meaning. For example, a 9-year-old child recently reported, "I'm making my mother some place to put her *sooz.*" It seemed logical enough to interpret this description as a shoe bag; following much discussion and frustration, however, it was ascertained that the child meant *spools* and, in fact, that she was making her mother a spool holder.

Children who do not understand the meaning of words experience problems in decoding semantics. They may lack knowledge of the concepts represented by words or have had no experience with the relevant vocabulary. Sometimes, the relation between semantics and syntax is very close, which complicates the problem and affects both the decoding and encoding processes. For example, to understand *wh* questions (what, who, where, whose, etc.) children must know the concepts represented by the interrogative words as well as the concepts underlying the structures that are used to respond to them. Specifically, the concept of time underlies comprehension of the word "when"; the response to a "when" question requires understanding of the adverbial, prepositional phrase and of tense structures. Similarly, a "where" question demands understanding of spatial concepts and adverbial and prepositional phrase structures as well (Yoder, 1974).

Problems in word retrieval, that is, word finding, word recall, or word formulation, affect semantic encoding. Sometimes children with these difficulties substitute one word for another, such as, "sticker" for stamp. At other times, they create new words that logically reflect their intent but cannot be understood outside of the context. For example, in trying to remember the word *letter* a child said "stimalope," as in stamp plus envelope. At times, children also may provide associative descriptions instead of the desired single word, as in the case of a child who responded, "Doors with a clock right on top," for elevator, and "Peoples in, they dead under," for grave.

Decoding syntax involves processing the sequential structural order of an utterance according to the established grammatical rules of the language. For example, the sentences, "The dog bit the boy" and "The boy bit the dog," contain the same words. It is the sequence of the words—the location of the *doer* relative to the *action* and the *receiver*—that determines the meaning. Children who have trouble decoding syntax are unable to interpret meanings on the basis of these rules. They also may demonstrate problems following sequential directions. However, it is usually difficult to determine whether these problems relate to a syntax disorder or lack of auditory attention, or to an inability to retain an auditory sequence sufficiently long to process and appropriately respond to it.

Although all children demonstrate syntactic deviations as they are learning to master adult grammatical forms, by 3 or 4 years of age they usually have achieved most of these rules. Children who have not done so persist in demonstrating problems with word order and grammatical structure, or syntactic encoding. A simple example is a 6-year-old child who persists in using "me" for "I." However, while describing a visit to a medical office an 8-year-old child reported, "I was at a nurse before 'cause they took x-rays." Also, in describing a phone that rang simultaneously at home and at her father's next-door office, she said, "You call him, it's a call at office too. Who call family's phone it go upstairs and downstairs." These, of course are extreme examples, but they clearly illustrate the effects of the problem on communication.

In summary, consideration of language problems should include attention to (a) linguistic processes (decoding and encoding), and (b) linguistic components (phonology, semantics, and syntax), and (c) the conceptual or referential system represented by observable language behavior. It also must account for the interdependency of the linguistic components and processes and the relation between the linguistic and conceptual systems.

Multiple Communicative Problems

It has been pointed out that the various types of verbal communicative problems are not mutually exclusive. A given child may demonstrate several aspects of one type of problem, several types of problems, or both. Multiple communicative problems are particularly common among children with special education needs whose speech and language defects are one aspect of more general physical, intellectual, emotional, social, behavioral, and/or motor problems.

CHILDREN WITH CLEFT PALATES

20

Children who are at high risk for multiple communicative problems but who, as a group, do not usually require special academic considerations, are those born with cleft palates. The cleft may extend from the lip to the gum ridge, hard palate, and soft palate, or any combination, on one or both sides of the mouth. Although the children's health, dental, and cosmetic problems also require attention, from the standpoint of verbal communication it is most important that the children undergo surgery and/or prosthetic management to provide them with potentially adequate speech mechanisms, otherwise, no amount of speech training is helpful.

Even following medical treatment some children are unable to close the passage between the nose and the mouth, normally accomplished by elevating the soft palate to contact the back of the throat wall. This closure is necessary for the production of sounds, with the exception of *m, n,* and *ng.* When children cannot achieve the closure, air and sound escape through the nose, affecting speech. If the lack of closure is based on habit rather than inadequate physical structures, speech training usually is helpful.

Children with incomplete closure, sometimes caused by a palatal insufficiency rather than a cleft, characteristically demonstrate a hypernasal voice quality and excessive nasal emission of air. They also demonstrate articulatory errors because they are unable to build up sufficient intra-oral pressure to shape and project the sounds through the mouth. Air escapes through the nose as they attempt to produce sounds. Also, they tend to retract the tongue, attempting to reduce the size of the escape passage, further complicating articulation. It is not uncommon for children with cleft palates to experience intermittent hearing losses, secondary to frequent upper respiratory infections, that also interfere with the ability to differentiate sounds and monitor speech.

Classroom teachers should understand the nature of these problems and their implications. The children's physical disfigurements, medical and dental problems, and poor speech may adversely affect their social and behavioral adjustment. In addition, it is important to realize that if the speech mechanism lacks the capability or potential for closing the passage, speech training is usually unwarranted.

21

HEARING-IMPAIRED CHILDREN

The type and severity of a hearing loss determine the effect on verbal communication. Children with permanent, severe hearing impairments are likely to demonstrate problems in all areas of verbal communication. Initially, their inability to hear interferes with speech-sound development. Later, even if they wear hearing aids for amplification and are taught to produce sounds, the children frequently do not hear well enough to self-monitor their articulation auditorally. They constantly must make an effort to speak as carefully as possible because they cannot hear their own verbal output. These children also may demonstrate high-pitched monotonous voice qualities.

They do not hear inflectional changes and are unaware that stress and rhythm can be varied.

Children with severe hearing losses tend to demonstrate a variety of language problems. They have difficulty with abstractions like humor, double meanings, and sarcasm. They must be taught syntactic rules since their hearing losses preclude their internalizing the rules naturally. They rely substantially on visual cues for language input and regularly miss segments of what is being said. Because of their difficulties with comprehending spoken language and speaking, they tend to fall several years behind in the linguistic skills necessary for academic achievement.

Children with moderate hearing losses, whose hearing aids provide them with reasonable amplification, demonstrate some of the same problems to a lesser degree. Since they are able to receive language input and self-monitor their output, their verbal communicative problems and subsequent academic problems frequently are reduced. Finally, children with mild hearing losses may have minor speech and language deviations. They often hear well enough for social speech purposes and miss only occasional sounds or sentences.

Classroom teachers can take certain measures for the benefit of children with hearing impairments. Some suggestions follow:

1. Learn how to determine whether a child's hearing aid is working. Speech-language pathologists, parents, educational audiologists, or teacher consultants in deaf education can provide the necessary instruction.

2. At the beginning of each class, check or remind the child to check that his or her hearing aid is working. Amplification is essential, particularly for children whose hearing acuity is substantially improved by it.

3. Seat a child with a hearing impairment so that he/she can see the teacher with as little effort as possible (preferential seating).

4. Avoid standing with your back to the light. It is difficult to speech read (lip read) under such circumstances.

5. Tell the child the topic under discussion and announce each change in topic. It is easier for a child to understand language and keep up with the flow of information if the subject is known.

6. Avoid talking while facing the blackboard, or turn and repeat what you said.

Mainstreaming hearing-impaired children has been a relatively long-term practice that continues to grow. Teachers, therefore, should be prepared to cope with hearing-impaired children in their classes.

CEREBRAL PALSIED CHILDREN

Cerebral palsied children demonstrate a range of speech and language problems, depending on the severity of the physical involvement and the degree to which the vocal and articulatory mechanisms are affected. Obviously, if the speech mechanisms are intact, a child may demonstrate no verbal problem at all. However, in some cases the child's ability to coordinate the muscles required for voice and speech is so poor that he or she is unable to produce a sustained tone or shape articulate sounds. In this instance, alternative modes of communication— speech synthesizers, communication boards, writing, typing, other symbol systems, sign language—are necessary.

Many cerebral palsied children who are able to speak demonstrate a cluster of symptoms called *dysarthria,* a speech difficulty secondary to neuromuscular problems. The children's symptoms include slow, labored articulation, a measured rate, monotony, and hypernasality. They are unable to make rapid sequential muscular adjustments in the speech mechanism and frequently slur their sounds. They do best when given encouragement, emotional support, and adequate time to mobilize their forces.

OTHER SPECIAL EDUCATION POPULATIONS

The incidence of speech and language problems tends to run high among children who have been categorized for educational purposes as mentally retarded, learning disabled, or emotionally disturbed. This circumstance is not surprising because the physical and psychopathological forces responsible for their general conditions also interfere with the mastery of auditory-verbal skills, the basis of academic achievement.

Educational classifications, however, do not define the unique linguistic needs of the children within each category or across categories. The speech and language needs of any group of children are as specific and different as each child within the group. Teachers, speech-language pathologists, and other school personnel, consequently, must evaluate each as an individual and design a remedial program specific to his/her needs.

Dialectal Differences

Dialectal differences cannot be construed as speech or language disorders. They are deviations from Standard American English which are based on the rules of the dialect, not on the speaker's ability to understand or speak. They reflect the internalization of the language rules of a primary culture or subculture.

As rule-governed systems, dialects differ from language and other dialects in any of the linguistic dimensions—phonological, semantic, or syntactic. At the phonological level, for example, the black dialect may systematically substitute d/th ("dem"/them) and omit "r" ("foe"/four). Semantically, the dialectal use of the word "bad" sometimes means nice or good, the opposite of Standard American English ("Dat's really bad"/That's really good). Finally, the syntax of a dialect may avoid redundancy in number designations. Therefore, "I have two sister(s)" is grammatically correct; there is no need to decline the noun, as plurality is already designated by the word "two."

It is important for teachers, school speech-language pathologists, and others to become sensitive to the rules of the dialects used by children and not to mistake dialectal rule differences for communicative deviations or disorders.

III

SPEECH AND LANGUAGE SERVICES

School speech and language programs usually consist of three major service components: identification, evaluation, and remediation. Each component includes a variety of activities that involve teacher participation. In fact, the success of speech and language programs largely depends on the interdisciplinary cooperation of teachers and speech-language pathologists.

Identification

The usual methods of identifying children with communicative problems are (a) screening and (b) teacher referrals. Some speech-language pathologists conduct annual screening programs that require brief and direct interactions with all kindergarten and older children who are new to a school district. Early in the school year, the speech-language pathologists interview the children to detect possible communicative problems. The screening procedures may consist of engaging the children in conversation and judging their communicative skills on the basis of their spontaneous language, or administering standardized tests which sample various aspects of speech and language or both.

As a result of federal and state legislation that mandates special education for children below age 5, many school districts have instituted comprehensive *preschool* screening programs. These programs involve early identification of cognitive, motor, and communicative problems. Depending on the philosophy of the district, the programs entail (a) administration of a single test battery, such as the Denver Development Screening Test (Frankenburg & Dodds, 1968), or the Developmental Indicators for the Assessment of Learning (Mardell & Goldenberg, 1975); (b) structured observations and testing of children by a school interdisciplinary team that includes psychologists, speech and language pathologists, nurses, early childhood specialists, teachers, and other relevant personnel; or (c) team observations of children in a natural play environment.

Under any circumstances, screening procedures are subject to a certain amount of error. They may fail to identify some children with problems and misidentify others. Consequently, the role of classroom teachers in verifying the presence or absence of problems is extremely important. In regard to communicative difficulties, for example, speech-language pathologists rely on teachers to observe and assess children's daily verbal behavior in various social and academic contexts. The data supplied by the teachers are then used to substantiate or refute the presence of a bona fide problem.

Some speech-language pathologists do not conduct screening programs. Instead, they depend totally on teachers to identify and refer children with possible or actual communicative problems. This circumstance places even greater responsibility on teachers to become familiar with the nature of speech development and its disorders and to ensure that children in need are referred for further evaluation.

Evaluation

Speech-language pathologists are responsible for the evaluation of the verbal communicative skills of children who are identified as having potential problems. The main objective of these evaluations is to collect data that can be used to develop individual remedial plans. These data generally include (a) information on etiologic or causative factors and (b) descriptions of the children's linguistic capabilities and weaknesses.

Identification of the causes of communicative problems is essential for at least three reasons: (a) Parents want to know why their children are having difficulty, and it is the responsibility of professionals to help them to find the answers. (b) The findings may indicate that medical and/or social-emotional intervention is needed to reduce or eliminate etiologic factors. (c) From an academic standpoint it is helpful to establish relations between known conditions and observable behaviors. The importance of etiology is sometimes overemphasized in schools, however, and should be placed in a more realistic perspective of its educational value. For example, etiologic findings commonly are used to categorize children for educational purposes (learning disabled, mentally retarded, emotionally disturbed, etc.), and the assumption is made that the children within a given classification share the same linguistic needs. In fact, however, the speech and language needs of each child within a category are unique; they are as different and specific as the individual. Furthermore, the classificatory labels, in and of themselves, frequently do not denote the causes of the problem or indicate a similarity in etiologic underpinnings from person to person. For instance, to say that a communicative disorder is secondary to a learning disability or to mental retardation merely qualifies one descriptive term with another, and fails to delineate the causes of either condition.

The most important outcomes of the evaluation for educational purposes, therefore, are descriptions of the children's linguistic proclivities and weaknesses. These descriptions provide a behavioristic base for determining what children are able to do rather than what they are considered to be. The descriptions contain information which can be translated into individual remedial programs.

Comprehensive speech and language evaluations require the collection and coordination of data obtained through (a) case histories, (b) specialized standardized tests and procedures, and (c) observations of behavior.

Speech-language pathologists, therefore, must interact directly with children, their parents, teachers, and other school specialists to obtain the evaluative information necessary for program planning.

CASE HISTORY

The scope and depth of a case history vary in accord with the type and severity of the presenting communicative problems. For example, most school speech-language pathologists would agree that it is less critical to have a complete history on a third-grade, well-adjusted achiever with an interdental lisp than a hard-of-hearing kindergartner with a repaired cleft palate, or an underachieving first grader with severely delayed speech and language development. However, particularly for children with moderate to severe communicative disorders, speech-language pathologists require information regarding birth history, developmental landmarks, specific stages of speech and language acquisition, medical history, school progress, and familial tendencies. These data are used to establish etiologic probabilities and to compare the children's patterns of speech and language development with their development in other areas. The information may be obtained by requesting parents to complete a written case history form, conducting a personal interview with them, or both.

Speech-language pathologists are also concerned about parents' attitudes toward their children's communicative problems. For this information, teachers also can be very helpful. They frequently have had regular interactions with the parents of problem children and know a great deal about the family situations. Teachers are able to contribute information about parental insights, attitudes, and feelings about the problems. They are able to assess the parents' willingness and ability to become involved in the remedial process. Teachers also tend to be sensitive to environmental factors that precipitate or perpetuate communicative difficulties, impressions that are critical to the speech-language pathologist's program of parent counseling.

Finally, teachers are an important source of information regarding the children's feelings about and attitudes toward their communicative problems and the effects of these problems on academic achievement and social adjustment. As a result of the problems and their ramifications, teachers frequently know which approaches and management techniques may be successful with problem children in the classroom, approaches that may be transferred to the remedial setting. In sum, as the central school figures in children's lives, teachers are an important link to understanding the history of their students' communicative problems.

STANDARDIZED TESTS AND PROCEDURES

There is no single test or instrument that measures primary linguistic skills. As a result, it is necesary for speech-language pathologists to use a variety of tests and techniques to assess the components of language behavior. The speech-language pathologists may piece together protocols that facilitate identifying some of the children's linguistic strengths and weaknesses but may fall short of providing measures of total language function. 29

A comprehensive speech and language evaluation considers (a) the linguistic code—its processes (decoding and encoding) and components (phonology, semantics, syntax)—and (b) the conceptual system represented by observable language behavior. A useful model for assessment of the linguistic code facilitates consideration of each process by component (Freeman, 1977). It is organized to assess children's ability to *decode* phonology, semantics, and syntax, as well as to *encode* each of these three components, providing six cells of information (Fig. 1).

Some tests have been developed to measure a single process-component, such as decoding phonemes or encoding syntax, while others measure several process-component pairs. For example, a test that demands verbal responses to verbal questions may be used, first, to tap decoding-semantics, then to measure encoding-syntax. Although the selection and use of specific tests depend on the background,

Linguistic Components	Process	
	Decoding	Encoding
Phonological	1	2
Semantic	3	4
Syntactic	5	6

Fig. 1. Scheme for organization of linguistic evaluative data.

training, and experience of given speech-language pathologists, the organization of obtained data into a process-by-component scheme permits all concerned professionals to (a) look at various dimensions of speech and language behavior, (b) establish baseline behaviors for linguistic components, and (c) analyze the process-component relation as involved in linguistic tasks. (See the Appendix for representative tests.)

Phonological Decoding

Auditory discrimination tests typically are used as the principle means of evaluating children's phonological decoding skills. These tests require children to differentiate pairs of words or syllables that contain a single phonemic variant. In some instances, the evaluator reads the paired stimuli aloud and the children indicate if the utterances are the same or different; in others, the children are asked to select a stimulus picture, the name of which is phonemically similar to the name of one of the surrounding foils. The basic skill required in either of these activities is differentiation of the phonemic structures of the spoken stimuli, broadly interpreted as phonological decoding.

Phonological Encoding

Phonetic inventories or tests of articulation evaluate the ability of children to produce sounds, or phonological encoding. Unlike others in the language battery, these tests are the sole territorial right of speech-language pathologists, usually the only members of a school staff with specific training in phonetics and phonetic transcription.

Tests of articulation consist of series of pictures designed to elicit the names of objects or action words that contain the various English speech sounds and combinations. Many of the tests also include "conversation cards," which are used to elicit connected speech. Speech-language pathologists use the data from tests of articulation, phonetic analyses of conversational speech samples, and evaluations of the children's ability to imitate isolated consonant and vowel sounds to assess children's phonological encoding skills.

Semantic Decoding

Picture vocabulary tests are the most popular means of evaluating children's semantic decoding skills. These tests consist of stimulus pictures surrounded by a group of foils. In response to verbal directions, children are asked to select the pictorial representation of each stimulus word.

Semantic Encoding

The ability of children to name pictures constitutes an aspect of semantic encoding that frequently is tested. The evaluator elicits the names of a graded series of pictures. The purpose is to measure the level of the children's verbal vocabulary.

Syntactic Decoding

Tests have been developed to assess skills in syntactic decoding. They require children to identify pictures that depict a variety of linguistic structures. For example, the children may be asked to point to "Ball on the table," "Happy boy sitting under the tree," or "Mother is being kissed by the baby." These tests relate to children's ability to comprehend the rules of word order.

Syntactic Encoding

Tests designed to assess syntactic encoding require children to repeat sequences of linguistic elements, with or without pictorial cues. Many speech-language pathologists also analyze children's spontaneous language samples

31

to determine their facility to use age-appropriate syntactic forms.

LIMITATIONS OF STANDARDIZED TESTS

1. Standardized speech and language tests and procedures are useful means of obtaining data about children's levels of linguistic performances on specific tasks. As in the case of etiologic factors, however, the importance of test scores sometimes is overrated and must be placed in a realistic perspective of educational significance. Although numerical scores per se are useful to identify or corroborate areas of linguistic strengths and weaknesses, they fail to reflect children's specific skills—the behaviors that underlie the achievement of scores. Yet, an analysis of these subskills often is more relevant to program planning than a series of numerical scores.

2. The validity of formal speech and language tests is an important concern. Because of the complexities and integrative aspects of auditory-verbal behavior, circumscribed linguistic processes or functions are frequently impossible to test, even if the title of a test indicates such a purpose. For example, although an auditory discrimination test may require children's differentiating two rhyming words with a single phonemic variant, this task also involves auditory acuity (ability to hear), auditory memory (ability to retain the signals sufficiently long to compare them), and understanding of the concepts "same" and "different." Therefore, the fact that a child fails to perform at age-level expectations on such a test may be important, although in itself the performance is insufficient evidence to regard the problem as restricted to auditory discrimination.

Similarly, tests designed to evaluate children's ability to decode syntax necessarily consist of sequenced linguistic elements. Although their primary intent is to assess children's ability to process and understand various linguistic structures, such tests also involve auditory attention, verbal comprehension, and auditory sequencing. These factors must be considered as carefully as the test scores before concluding that failure constitutes a deficiency in syntactic comprehension.

3. Most speech and language tests or procedures do not purport to assess all aspects of a given linguistic component-process. However, professionals tend to refer to scores on these tests as indicative of strengths or deficiencies in entire areas, as if they had been completely evaluated. For example, scores on picture vocabulary tests actually indicate the level at which children are able to match the names of objects or actions to pictorial representations. Although this task requires understanding of the stimulus words, it obviously does not include all aspects of semantic decoding. It should not be said, therefore, that the test scores are representative of "language comprehension."

4. The tendency of school personnel to rely on standardized speech and language tests to demonstrate professional accountability is a matter of concern. Although it may seem logical to use a pre-test—intervention—post-test model to measure children's progress, this system often is superficial. It may reflect that the children have been taught to perform the tasks on a test rather than to internalize and generalize pragmatic linguistic principles.

A further complication is created when the test items are far removed from the actual demands of every-day communication. For example, a popular method of evaluating children's auditory sequencing abilities is based on the repetition of progressively longer series of digits, forward and backward. Not only is this a relatively nonessential communicative task but the relevance of coping satisfactorily with sequences of digits as opposed to sequences of words in a phrase or sentence has not been established. Similarly, during picture identification tests, children may be asked to point to actions—"Show me hopping"—a construction that normally is not used in conversational speech.

5. A number of artifacts that enter into testing situations must be considered before drawing conclusions from

scores: (a) The limited sample of speech and language behavior observed in evaluative sessions may not reflect children's typical and varied linguistic performances. (b) The variability among evaluators who administer tests is difficult to control. (c) The populations of children on whom procedures have been standardized may be biased with respect to a given child. (d) Children with language problems may not understand the directions and may try to fake their way through evaluative procedures.

Despite these limitations, standardized speech and language tests provide basic information on children's levels of linguistic performance. When appropriately interpreted, the tests indicate areas that should be probed further through diagnostic teaching, observations, and additional formal evaluations. However, test results generally focus only on the linguistic code or symbolic representations used by children. Additional strategies must be employed to gain insights into the underlying conceptual or referential systems.

34

EVALUATION OF THE CONCEPTUAL SYSTEM

Breakdowns in the linguistic code used by children are sometimes based on inadequate conceptual development. At one level, a problem may involve a child's insufficient experiential background to support correct labeling (e.g., the child may call all animals "dog"); at another level, the problem may reflect the child's lack of the concepts of linguistic structures (e.g., the child is unable to identify the actor in the statement, "The boy was hit by the girl," because he or she does not understand the passive structure). Evaluation of these kinds of relations between children's conceptual systems and the linguistic code require an ongoing assessment of the children's language-related processes.

A procedural model for this type of assessment may be derived from language-learning theorists who have stated that (a) sensorimotor experiences and perceptions of these experiences are contingencies to concept development and (b) many words come to stand for or to name concepts that were learned preverbally (Carroll, 1964, Chappell, 1977; Clark, 1974; Richardson, 1967). Under these circumstances, the basic processes involved in language development, although interrelated, may be identified as reception, perception, conceptualization, and verbalization. From an educationally pragmatic viewpoint, (a) reception involves sensory intactness or the ability to receive stimuli through the end organs, (b) perception refers to the ability to distinguish the finite physical characteristics or attributes of stimuli once they have been received, (c) conceptualization requires the ability to group stimuli according to their universally perceived similarities of properties or attributes, and (d) verbalization refers to the assignment of names to concepts (Freeman, 1977).

Despite the interrelation of these processes, it is practical to evaluate children with language problems in terms of the predominance of the processing difficulties they seem to demonstrate. Speech-language pathologists, therefore, are concerned with evaluative data that are suggestive of breakdowns in one or several of these processes. Because it is postulated that these difficulties interfere with language learning, information about them is basic to the organization of remedial strategies and programs.

OBSERVATIONS OF BEHAVIOR

The credibility of objective observations of behavior as valid evaluative determinants must be re-established among school speech-language pathologists. Because of the emphasis that most school districts place on the use of standardized tests, speech-language pathologists often have succumbed to the educational test craze of the past 15 years. School specialists, teachers, and administrators have come to expect reports of speech and language test scores to take precedence over other data, whether the scores are or are not most relevant to child-management practices. This circumstance is particularly unfortunate in the case of children with verbal communicative problems.

35

As already indicated, even if speech-language pathologists were to administer all available tests to a child with a primary language difficulty, the end results would fall short of an adequate picture of the child's linguistic skills. Consequently, a valid speech and language evaluation also must consider recorded observations of children's spontaneous communication in natural environments. In the last analysis, it is the effectiveness of communication under these circumstances that is of ultimate importance. Therefore, the observations of teachers, speech-language pathologists, and parents should be regarded as an integral part of the evaluation.

Sometimes, children respond to test items in an unanticipated manner. Their responses may be different from those expected by the test constructors and, hence, cannot be scored in the standardized way. However, an analysis of these responses may be more important to program planning than the anticipated scores. Therefore, descriptions of the children's behavior should be recorded accurately and objectively for use as additional evaluative data. In essence, speech-language pathologists do well, at times, to use tests as a means of observing rather than measuring communicative behavior. For example, during administration of a picture vocabulary test, a child may ignore the evaluator's request to point to the stimulus pictures and, instead, will describe all the pictures on a page. The skilled evaluator captures these reponses as data on which to base an evaluation of semantic-encoding. Similarly, when nonverbal children use gestures to respond to questions, the evaluators can record and interpret these gestures as a means of assessing the children's knowledge and understanding.

Finally, evaluation of the conceptual system, as described earlier, largely depends on observations. The essential aspect of this procedure is not the test or series of items used to evaluate specific language-related areas, but the organization of responses in terms of their possible relations to language processes. Therefore, teachers and parents contribute essential evaluative information when they report their observations of children's abilities to receive, perceive, conceptualize, and verbalize information. In sum, although speech-language pathologists assume the major responsibility for evaluating children's verbal communicative skills, classroom teachers have an important role in each aspect of the process. Teachers may (a) share historical information that is critical to understanding the nature of the children and their problems, (b) gain an understanding of the nature, value, and limitations of standardized speech and language tests within an appropriate educational perspective, and (c) contribute their observations of children's communicative behavior to the collection of data that are necessary for assessment and remedial planning.

Although formal evaluations of speech and language problems usually are conducted in only one or two sessions, the process of assessment continues throughout case management. Children's responses to remedial programs constitute ongoing evaluative information about their linguistic strengths and weaknesses, the appropriateness of the programs, and the need for program modifications. Evaluation, therefore, is inseparable from remediation.

Remediation

The main purpose of speech and language programs is to enable children to modify their verbal communicative behavior. Since each child's communicative problem is different, however, speech-language pathologists must use the results of initial evaluations to organize and implement individualized programs to meet the range of needs and to identify specific target behaviors for modification. The range may extend from indirect environmental support for children with normal maturational speech and language differences to very intensive, direct speech and language remediation for children with severe communicative disorders.

In response to the wide range of service needs in schools, ASHA has recommended that comprehensive speech and language programs be organized along a continuum (Healey, 1974). The key points of this continuum are (a) a communicative development component at one end, (b) a communicative deviations component in the middle, and (c) a communicative disorders component at the other end (Fig. 2). The continuum acommodates the verbal communicative needs of all children in a district.

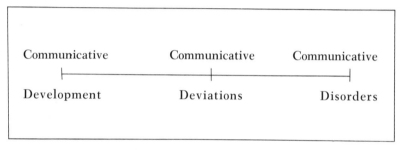

Communicative   Communicative   Communicative

Development   Deviations   Disorders

Fig. 2. Continuum of school speech and language services.

COMMUNICATIVE DEVELOPMENT

The development of auditory-verbal skills is basic to academic achievement. Since, among school staffs, the speech-language pathologists usually have had the most training and experience in this area, they should participate actively in a district's communicative development program. In addition, because these programs facilitate the improvement of all children's primary linguistic skills, they prevent the development of communicative problems, a primary concern of speech-language pathologists.

As part of the communicative development program, speech-language pathologists should work with teachers and curriculum specialists to organize and present sequenced curricular activities that address the specific needs of early elementary-school-aged children in a given school. For example, if a school speech-language pathologist and a teacher identify a group of kindergarten children who demonstrate difficulty with "wh" questions, the professionals must determine if the children's problems relate to inadequate understanding of the concepts underlying the interrogative words, syntax deficiencies, or both. In the first case, the curriculum planned would include activities for the development of time (when), space (where), possession (whose), and related concepts; in the second case, curricular activities with a developmental syntax approach would be instituted (Lee, Koenigsnecht, & Mulhern, 1975).

If necessary, speech-language pathologists may provide periodic demonstration lessons and sustained consultative support to curricular programs. However, once the children's major needs are identified and the programs are developed, classroom teachers should implement them. Since children who demonstrate linguistic inadequacies at the auditory-verbal level have a weak foundation for reading and writing, the development of the primary linguistic skills is an essential aspect of their basic education and belongs in the classroom.

A major responsibility of speech-language pathologists in communicative development is making teachers and parents aware of the factors that prevent auditory-verbal problems. For example, in today's child-pressuring society, it is important that speech-language pathologists continuously emphasize that many children's early speech deviations are maturational and normal. Premature and undue pressure to correct these errors may lead to negative feelings about communication, personal or social maladjustment, or other attendant school and home problems.

In the development of auditory-verbal skills it is very easy for parents and teachers to provide stimulation and demand responses that are several levels above children's actual capabilities. This practice encourages children to leap from an observable level of performance to a superficial display of desired behavior, instead of progressing to the target through incremental units. Thus the outcomes include, for example, rote counting instead of awareness of a one-to-one correspondence, programed answers to questions that are not understood, and ignorance of the fact, until much later, that "lmnop" is not one letter.

In order to promote the prevention of communicative problems through positive environmental support, speech-language pathologists should encourage parents and teachers to use such techniques as (a) repeating what children have said and modeling and expanding their utterances, without placing pressure on the children to follow suit, (b) limiting the steps in a given direction to accord reasonably with the children's maturational level, (c) permitting children to talk and listening to them without interruption, thereby encouraging them to listen, (d) offering children verbal choices when they seem in doubt, (e) attempting to second guess the context of an incomprehensible message before asking a child to repeat it, and (f) accepting maturational speech and language errors as normal.

COMMUNICATIVE DEVIATIONS

40

The communicative deviations component of a speech and language program is designed to meet the needs of children with mild to moderate auditory-verbal differences. Some of these children may be experiencing slow maturation while others may demonstrate a limited number of well-established maladaptive behaviors that deviate from the norm. For example, a third-grade child may persist in substituting "w"/"r" and "l" but have no other difficulty; another child may demonstrate a lateral lisp only on the "s" and "z" sounds.

In the past, many school speech-language pathologists invested a majority of their time in what is now called the "communicative deviations component." They provided direct service to large numbers of children with mild to moderate deviations, a substantial percentage of which were articulatory errors. They generally worked directly with these children in biweekly, small-group sessions of 20-30 minutes in length. In addition, the speech-language pathologists indirectly served the children by consulting with their parents and teachers about speech improvement techniques and activities that could be carried on at home and in the classroom.

As more communicative development components have been established to meet the needs of larger numbers of children with minor and maturational speech and language errors, speech-language pathologists have been able to decrease their over-all time allotment to the communicative deviations component and to increase the time they spend with children whose speech deviations actually require direct attention. These latter children frequently need to be (a) taught a specific skill or set of skills, (b) provided with opportunities to practice these skills in controlled situations, and (c) monitored in their use of the new skills in social and academic contexts. They require more than the indirect approach of a preventive program although less than the intensive contact demanded for severe communicative disorders

Children often use their new communicative skills consistently in the confines of the speech class but revert to their old habit patterns when they walk out of the room. Teachers, therefore, are an important part of the carry-over process, that is, they can be particularly helpful in assisting children to carry their newly acquired speech and language skills from the speech class into the regular classroom. Teachers should (a) be aware of children's new habit patterns in order to reinforce and reward their spontaneous use, (b) offer appropriate reminders to the children to use their new skills, (c) provide indirect correction through modeling, (d) participate in the use of carry-over devices, such as tracking charts, which are designed by the children and speech-language pathologists to serve as reminders, and (e) capitalize on routine classroom activities as opportunities for children to practice specific verbal skills.

COMMUNICATIVE DISORDERS

Children with severe articulation, voice, fluency, or language problems require intensive intervention. Their communicative disorders interfere with academic achievement and social adjustment and frequently are secondary to more general physical, intellectual, or emotional problems. It often is necessary to coordinate the efforts of several special service professionals, teachers, and aides to meet their complex needs.

As members of school teams, speech-language pathologists should be expected to contribute to the development of appropriate remedial-educational programs for children with communicative disorders. The speech-language pathologists should (a) provide a comprehensive summary of each child's linguistic competencies, (b) identify and interpret relations between the child's linguistic competency and performance on psychological and educational assessment, and (c) relate the child's learning patterns in linguistic skills to the academic demands of the classroom (Robertson & Freeman, 1974). Each of these responsibilities overlaps those of classroom teachers.

42   To stress the need for cooperation between speech-language pathologists and teachers in the evaluation of children's communicative disorders, it must be kept in mind that comprehensive summaries of children's linguistic competencies are not totally reflected in scores. These summaries also should include behavioral descriptions in language that is understandable to all team members and, most important, to teachers, who are in the position to corroborate or refute their reliability. If necessary, teachers should request the restatement of unclear information; they should not be intimidated by esoteric vocabulary or the names of tests with which they are not familiar.

Classroom teachers should familiarize speech-language pathologists with the various achievement tests and educational instruments that they routinely use. Inasmuch as children with communicative disorders are frequently least able to perform well on standardized tests that depend substantially on linguistic skills, and many do, it is essential that speech-language pathologists interrelate their findings with other test results to highlight the effects of the communicative disorders on the children's performances. For example, if teachers administer language-weighted tests to children with communicative disorders, speech-language pathologists should be prepared to interpret the effects of the children's disorders on the scores as well as on the responses to specific test items. Similarly, if tests include both verbal and performance items, the speech-language pathologists should be able to discuss the ramifications of marked differences in responses between the two areas, as well as the significance of a scatter of scores among the subtests in either area. Speech-language pathologists also should validate the children's understanding of concepts required by test directions.

Finally, speech-language pathologists and teachers should share information on children's learning patterns, including their reactions to learning situations, the extent to which their communicative disorders seem to be affecting these reactions, and the possible relation of other behavioral tendencies to learning. For example, when the problems of children with communicative disorders consistently interfere with the ability to follow the successive stages of teachers' directions, the children may demonstrate secondary defensive reactions that superficially appear to be inappropriate classroom behavior. Discussions between speech-language pathologists and teachers regarding such children could lead to jointly planned strategies to rectify this type of situation and increase learning probabilities. Strategies might include (a) shortening directions, (b) providing one stage of directions at a time, or (c) rephrasing the directions and, at the same time, conducting a specific remedial program to improve the children's listening skills. Both speech-language pathologists and teachers are concerned with the individual characteristics of children and the application of principles and theories of learning that recognize those characteristics. The professionals should support each other in this common goal.

43

Implementing Services

The implementation of a continuum of speech and language services requires a number of alterations in the traditional itinerant program. These changes include (a) establishing a new priority system of case-load selection, (b) distributing services according to children's needs rather than the population size of school buildings, and (c) instituting a variety of service and scheduling models. Needless to say, such changes demand adjustments on the part of school principals, classroom teachers, and speech-language pathologists. It is particularly important that teachers understand and support the changes because, as with other departures from established school routines, they are likely to be most affected.

CASE-LOAD SELECTION

A priority system of case-load selection is essential to the provision of a continuum of speech and language services. Zemmol (1977) described a system that reviews children with communicative problems along a continuum of *need* that parallels that of *services*. In this system, first priority is given to children whose needs correspond to the communicative disorders component, second priority, to those in the communicative deviations component, and third priority, to those in the communicative development component. In addition, a component of consultative services is added for children who do not require regularly scheduled sessions. Activities associated with prevention are included in this component.

In implementing such a system, speech-language pathologists must so allocate their available time that the children with the highest priority receive the most attention. As the children progress, their priority ratings are changed and they are moved through the continuum of service components until, ultimately, they are dismissed. This system is child-centered. It does not rely on teacher convenience (e.g., scheduling all children in a given classroom for remediation at the same time). Instead, it demands flexibility in the children's routines as well as in speech-language pathologists' schedules. It facilitates remedial sessions as they are needed—as often as every day, or as infrequently as once a month—and, thus, requires the availability of a room in which speech-language pathologists can work. If its attendant problems can be resolved, the system offers a rational, defensible, professionally sound program structure that is responsive to the needs of children.

Another change required by a continuum of services that is based on need is the elimination of the idea that every elementary building in a district is rightfully entitled to a certain amount of the speech-language pathologists' time. Despite the fact that the proportion of children with different degrees of communicative problems is not constant from one school to another, in some school systems it has become customary for speech and language service time to be distributed proportionately among all buildings according to the population distribution. This circumstance results in speech-language pathologists serving schools rather than children and inhibits the provision of services according to need.

45

VARYING SERVICE AND SCHEDULING MODELS

The delivery of a continuum of services requires adapting the program to the needs of each child rather than fitting children into an existing program structure. A continuum of services cannot be achieved by using a single scheduling model. The traditional biweekly itinerant schedule may be appropriate for some children but it provides too much or too little service to others. Instead, speech-language pathologists must use a variety of service and scheduling models according to children's needs. Typically, these models include itinerant services with optional individual or small-group intermittent sessions on a regular though not necessarily biweekly basis, or intensive cycling that provides daily services for a block of time, followed by a break, then another block of time. When speech-language pathologists are building based, that is, assigned to one building only, they are in a position to offer intermittent and intensive scheduling options along the entire continuum.

Another option covers situations in which two or more speech-language pathologists in a school system combine efforts to deliver services according to their personal strengths, competencies, and interests. As with all groups of professionals, few speech-language pathologists are equally capable in all areas of their jobs. Therefore, in districts where school buildings are fairly close, travel time is relatively short, and the number of staff members allows it, speech-language pathologists may consider functioning as a departmental team, matching their strengths to children's needs across school-building boundaries. Although this system breaks the regularity of scheduling, requiring speech-language pathologists to distribute themselves according to cases rather than schools, and requires principals and teachers to deal with more than one speech-language pathologist at a time, it is worthy of consideration as an alternative, appropriate service model.

Principles of Remediation

The specific strategies used to modify and improve children's communicative behaviors are as varied and numerous as the speech-language pathologists who employ them. For example, some speech-language pathologists center their case-management techniques around indirect games while others are more comfortable and successful with direct drill materials. In any event, the use of a specific technique usually depends on the likelihood that it will produce the desired results as well as the evaluation of its success.

Speech-language pathologists also vary in their use of learning models. Some have been trained to follow a stimulus-response-reward paradigm; others are well-versed in principles of behavior modification and structure their lessons strictly according to an operant conditioning model. Many are eclectic, adapting various practices to meet the unique circumstances of each situation. Despite these individual professional differences, however, most speech-language pathologists are on common ground regarding the general principles of remediation. For example, each (a) establishes the success level of children on specific linguistic skills, (b) identifies the target behaviors to be modified, (c) outlines incremental plans to facilitate the development of these behaviors, (d) implements these plans, and (e) modifies the plans to meet the children's changing needs. The plans progress from the gross to the fine, from the concrete to the abstract. They are organized in a sequential manner to insure that one skill is based on another and that each progressively leads to the established goal.

Regardless of the specific skill involved (e.g., modification of a speech sound, reduction in nasality, following a two-stage direction), management plans usually include (a) identification of the desired behavior, (b) isolation of the behavior, (c) mastery of the isolated behavior, (d) mastery of the behavior in a variety of communicative contexts in speech class, (e) transferring the skill to the regular classroom (carry-over), and (f) stabilizing the use of the skill in all situations. Obviously, the last two stages depend on classroom teachers' and parents' assistance in monitoring the children's newly acquired communicative habits until they are fully and consistently automated.

Finally, remediation depends on a team approach. It may involve speech-language pathologists, reading specialists, classroom teachers, psychologists, resource teachers, and other personnel. Since it requires team coordination regarding who is going to do what to whom, it should be based on the premise that the competencies of each member of a school staff will be integrated into a unified program to meet the presenting needs. This premise eliminates traditional professional territorial boundaries. It entails the delivery of the most comprehensive service by the most competent providers, whoever they may be. The premise requires matching a child's needs to the educator or educators who are best able to meet them. It necessitates case-centered, behaviorally based discussions among teachers, speech-language pathologists, and other personnel as each assists in the organization and implementation of an appropriate remedial plan.

PART 2

IV

CLASSROOM TEACHERS AND SPEECH AND LANGUAGE SERVICES

Relatively few school speech and language programs currently provide a complete, equally balanced continuum of services. This circumstance results from (a) a lack of uniformity among school districts in the concept of the role and responsibilities of speech-language pathologists, (b) differing educational philosophies from one district to another, and (c) variations in the priority assigned to speech and language programs.

Traditionally, speech-language pathologists primarily have served children with articulatory deviations, working with them in small groups for 20-30 minutes twice a week. Although the speech-language pathologists also have worked with some children whose problems are more severe, and have participated in occasional early elementary classroom-oriented speech improvement programs, these activities have been largely secondary. The core of the programs has been the speech deviations component.

The traditional, well-established program has involved the same speech-language pathologists at the same schools on the same schedules for many years. Thus, principals and teachers have known what to expect each year. The situation has been very comfortable with the services stable, predictable, and delivered as anticipated.

During recent years, as a result of concerted efforts by speech-language pathologists, their roles and responsibilities have been changing in some school districts. The speech-language pathologists are gaining recognition for their training and background in language development which exceeds those of other members of the school team. Therefore, elementary teachers who are concerned with language development are inclined to turn to the speech-language pathologists as resource consultants on language arts curricula. Similarly, as pressures have increased for schools to provide all handicapped children with equal and appropriate educational opportunities, and it has become more apparent that communicative disorders often are an integral component of these children's learning problems, the speech-language pathologists are being expected to provide more frequent and intensive services to children with the greatest needs.

These developments present a new challenge to those speech-language pathologists who are eager to broaden their services and, consequently, to alter their professional image. The changes firmly establish speech-language pathologists as important and even essential members of the educational team. However, principals and teachers must support the changes in administrative procedures that are necessary if speech-language pathologists are to institute new program components. These modifications frequently include (a) new schedules that are likely to create interruptions in the classroom more often than twice a week (previously, all "speech" children customarily were called out at the same time on a biweekly schedule); the new schedules are based on children's needs rather than convenience of grouping; (b) redistribution of the speech-language pathologists' time so that the greatest amount of service is given to those schools in which children have the greatest needs; (c) varied participation of classroom teachers across the whole range of the continuum of speech-language services; and (d) division of responsibilities among the speech-language pathology staff within a district according to their competencies and abilities. In short, speech-language pathologists must be willing to change their own patterns of operation; principals and teachers must be willing to accept these changes and the initial inconveniences created by them.

A second factor that sometimes interferes with the development of a full continuum of school speech-language services is educational philosophy. Some school districts have simply failed to acknowledge the relation between primary language skills and academic achievement. Their language arts curricula for all children, starting in the kindergarten, begin with reading. However, some early elementary curriculum consultants and teachers are convinced that comprehension of spoken language and speaking relate significantly to children's achievement in other language modes. These professionals are eager to work with speech-language pathologists to identify children's pre-reading needs, design programs to meet these needs, and implement these programs on a cooperative, interdisciplinary basis.

Finally, despite good intentions, and even when the program is judged to be of high priority, some school districts frankly lack the necessary financial resources to support the number of staff members that are needed for a full range of speech-language services. However, these circumstances may be changed in the future as a result of federal legislation and state mandatory special education laws; they require that children with special needs receive appropriate programs and services.

Model Programs

Despite the fact that relatively few school districts have been able to implement a fully developed continuum of speech-language services, many have established one or several exemplary components. In all instances these program components include the active participation of classroom teachers. For example, in the area of prevention, Stephenson (1974) described strategies for planning a kindergarten and first-grade program for the development of articulatory skills. He suggested coordinating the efforts of curriculum specialists, classroom teachers, and speech-language pathologists in the formulation of plans which can be integrated into daily classroom procedures with consultative assistance from the speech-language pathologists.

On the other end of the continuum, Knight (1974) reported methods to structure language remediation in special self-contained classrooms for early primary children with severe communicative deficits. After two years, when these children are returned to regular classrooms, language consultants can schedule them for individual remedial sessions. More frequently, however, the consultants observe the children in the classrooms and work with their teachers on materials and programs that can be used in the regular educational setting.

In order to demonstrate clearly additional realistic and practical ways in which classroom teachers in various administrative arrangements can participate in speech and language programs, some exemplary programs were visited to observe their practices and describe their major features. Together, these descriptions provide a set of adaptable models that represent numerous school district variants, as well as the entire span of speech and language services.

Site visits were made to six programs; two had a strong component for communicative development; two, a strong component for communicative deviations; and two, a strong component for communicative disorders. The data collected in each program were restricted to a single component although a given program may have been strong in several areas. Criteria for the selection of programs visited were as follows:

1. Published reports substantiating the cooperative efforts of speech-language pathologists and classroom teachers in the delivery of speech and language services.

2. Presentations at national conferences.
3. National reputation for team management of children with communicative deviations or disorders.
4. Accreditation by the Professional Services Board of the American Speech and Hearing Association.
5. Diverse geographic locations.
6. Diversified population densities (urban, suburban, rural).
7. Inclusion of minority populations.

The programs selected for visits were,
1. Mesa Public Schools, Mesa, Arizona;
2. Gouldsboro Grammar School, Gouldsboro, Maine;
3. Seattle Public Schools, Seattle, Washington;
4. Amherst-Pelham Regional Schools, Amherst, Massachusetts;
5. Special School District of Saint Louis County, Town and Country, Missouri; and
6. Greensboro Public Schools, Greensboro, North Carolina.

53

Each program was visited for two days during the spring of 1976. Interviews were held with administrators, teachers, speech-language pathologists, and other special service personnel. The critical part of each visit, however, was actual observation of the programs in action.

Although each program is unique, a number of factors can be identified that are common to all. They are as follows:
1. Administrators who are committed to
   ...meeting the individual educational needs of each child,
   ...promoting the concept that auditory-verbal skills are essential and basic to academic achievement,
   ...instituting experimental and innovative programs to achieve educational objectives, and

...applying an interdisciplinary model.
2. Classroom teachers who are committed to
   ...developing oral communication as an essential component of the language arts curriculum,
   ...altering their teaching practices and schedules to meet the individual auditory-verbal needs of each child,
   ...sharing critical case information with speech-language pathologists,
   ...gaining knowledge and learning new techniques and methods from speech-language pathologists,
   ...sharing knowledge, ideas, and methods with speech-language pathologists, and
   ...coordinating individual educational programs through interdisciplinary team-management practices.
3. Speech-language pathologists who are committed to
   ...developing programs that promote skills in all children,
   ...diversifying progams and scheduling practices to meet the individual needs of each child,
   ...sharing techniques and materials with classroom teachers,
   ...gaining knowledge and new techniques from classroom teachers,
   ...depending on teachers to participate actively in remedial speech and language programs, and
   ...improving services through experimentation, evaluation, and change.

The following descriptions are summaries of the highlights of the programs as they existed at the time. They describe what actually is happening, rather than what ought to be happening. The descriptions emphasize: (a) the interactions between classroom teachers and speech-language pathologists in the provision of exemplary speech and language services; (b) the role functions and expectations of each professional according to the service and scheduling practices in use; (c) the differences in expectations and responsibilities of classroom teachers in each type of service component; and (d) the classrooom teachers' responsibilities within each service component.

The unique circumstances in every school district make it impossible for any model to be replicated in every detail. However, each has adaptable elements that demonstrate effective ways in which teachers and speech-language pathologists cooperate in the delivery of speech and language services in the classroom. The descriptions of these programs may serve as springboards for school districts that are interested in planning, developing, and implementing a full complement of speech and language services.

V

EARLY INTERVENTION-PREVENTION PROGRAMS

Mesa Public Schools
Mesa, Arizona

An early intervention program for children with potential language-learning disabilities has been instituted at the Whitman School in Mesa, Arizona. This program is designed (a) to identify children with developmental deficits that are likely to interfere with academic achievement, and (b) to provide these children with supplementary programs that promote academic readiness. Speech and language services are a substantial component of the program.

Mesa, a city with about 103,000 residents, is located in the Phoenix area. The Mesa school district extends beyond the incorporated city limits onto two adjacent Indian reservations and encompasses an area of 200 square miles. The city supports 25 elementary schools, 6 junior high schools, 4 high schools, and a kindergarten class that is located on one of the reservations. Nine of the elementary schools include both self-contained and open-space classes; the others mainly have self-contained rooms.

About 28,500 students attend the Mesa Public Schools, of whom 15,000 are enrolled in the elementary grades (K-6). The minority group population is 18%: 15%, Mexican-American; 2%, black; and 1% American-Indian. The socio-economic range of the community is broad but predominantly middle class.

The Mesa schools have a comprehensive special education program. Self-contained classes as well as resource rooms are maintained within regular school buildings to provide flexibility to meet individual needs. The children in the self-contained rooms participate in classes or activities with other children in the school in a "modified mainstream" or integrated approach. Students in resource rooms attend regular classes except for the 1-3 hours per day that they receive instruction from the special education resource teachers. The district has been divided into regions to permit children with special needs to attend a school as close to home as possible.

The system employs 18 speech and language specialists. By and large, they conduct fairly traditional itinerant programs. However, in one building, the Whitman Elementary School, a full-time speech and language specialist is on the staff.

Whitman School Program

Whitman School serves 720 children (K-6). Most of its 23 classrooms are constructed in groups of four around a small, central atrium. A substantial amount of team teaching is practiced and the children are accustomed to moving to various stations during the day. Since 10-12% of the children come from low socio-economic homes, the school qualifies for federal funding under Title I. Partial support for the full-time speech and language specialist is provided by Title VI-G funds.

DEVELOPMENT OF THE KINDERGARTEN PROGRAM

During the 1974-1975 school year, the kindergarten teachers at the Whitman School noted that an inordinate number of students were not ready for first grade. This situation was critical in light of a school district policy that encourages promotion at the end of the kindergarten year. Consequently, the principal, speech and language specialist, learning disabilities specialist, and kindergarten teachers decided to organize a program to identify the characteristics of high-risk learning failures and to provide for the individual needs of children with such characteristics.

The first requirement was an appropriate screening procedure. After reviewing a number of instruments, the *Developmental Indicators for the Assessment of Learning* —DIAL (Mardell & Goldenberg, 1975)—was chosen. This instrument is designed to screen preschool children for gross and fine motor problems, problems in conceptual development, and communication difficulties.

With support from the Arizona State Department of Education, the authors of the DIAL were invited to conduct a workshop on the administration, scoring, and interpretation of the instrument. Subsequently, members of the Whitman staff administered the DIAL to the 115 children then enrolled in the kindergarten. Despite the fact that the test is designed for preschool children, 15% of Whitman's kindergartners scored below age-level expectations in at least one test area.

As a result, the following immediate measures were taken:

1. A physical education program was organized for the children who demonstrated difficulties in gross motor coordination. This program was implemented by the physical education teacher.

2. "Shoe Box" remediation kits were developed to teach individual skills, such as colors or copying shapes. These kits were used to provide two 30-minute periods of peer tutoring per week to children who demonstrated specific deficiencies. The sixth-grade students serving as tutors used the remediation kits under the direction, supervision, and monitoring of a learning disabilities resource teacher and the speech and language specialist.

3. The speech and language specialist conducted an in-depth assessment of those children who failed the concepts and communication skills subtests.

These evaluations revealed that speech and language development was normal in some of the children, despite poor performance on the DIAL. Other children demonstrated possible serious learning problems and were referred for psychological and educational evaluations with appropriate follow-up. A third group demonstrated the need for intensive speech and language intervention, which was provided.

4. The DIAL profiles of the children were reviewed to identify areas in which many children demonstrated deficiencies. The kindergarten teachers used this information to reorganize the curriculum to stress areas in which their groups showed weaknesses.

Prior to the beginning of the 1975-1976 school year, the staff at Whitman School trained seven additional teams to administer the DIAL. Each team consisted of a learning disabilities specialist, a psychologist, a psychometrist, a speech and language specialist, and a fifth member from any of these disciplines. During the second week of the school year these teams screened the 2200 kindergarten children enrolled throughout the school district. They found that approximately 20% of the children demonstrated potential language-learning problems.

Since then, all kindergarten teachers have been trained to use the Shoe Box remediation kits. Also, depending on the availability of personnel, a variety of interventive programs to meet the needs of high-risk children has been developed in different schools. These programs range from use of the Shoe Box kits only to use of the kits with one or several supplemental special education services. The program at the Whitman School is the most comprehensive.

OPERATION OF THE PROGRAM

At the beginning of the 1975-1976 school year, 89 kindergarten children at Whitman were identified as potential language-learning failures. Depending on their needs,

59

these children were enrolled in specific skill development programs. Supplementary physical education is provided for children with gross motor inadequacies; a learning disabilities specialist provides remedial services to children with poor, fine motor coordination; and the speech and language specialist works with children deficient in the area of concepts-communication. A given child may participate in one or several of these enrichment programs. Also, peer tutoring continues to be available in the classroom.

The speech and language and fine motor programs are housed in a resource room. It is a standard classroom which has been divided into centers for typing, listening, play, auditory activities, visual activities, and manipulative activities. During the morning and afternoon, the two specialists simultaneously work for 30-minute periods with groups of 4-6 children from regular classrooms. The groups are seen daily.

60   The objectives of the speech and language program are to enable the children (a) to classify objects and pictures of objects into groups according to color, shape, and function; (b) to follow verbal instructions that contain at least three sequential components; (c) to repeat a verbal stimulus of specified length; (d) to demonstrate sequential comprehension and recall of the essential details of a story; and (e) to comprehend and express concepts which are necessary for the first grade, as detailed on the *Boehm Test of Basic Concepts* (Boehm, 1971).

IMPLICATIONS FOR THE KINDERGARTEN TEACHER

As a result of this program, the kindergarten teachers have assumed greater responsibilities in educational assessment, curriculum development, and remediation of children's speech and language and specific learning deficits.

Because the DIAL is a screening instrument, some children with problems are missed and others are misidentified. The teachers validate the results obtained on the DIAL through observations and informal assessments of the children's classroom behaviors. Children who appear to need special education are referred for additional evaluations by appropriate specialists, whether they passed the DIAL or not. The classroom teachers have become increasingly sensitive to the needs of each child, recording objective observations that substantiate these needs, and sharing this information with other team members.

On the basis of group performances on the DIAL, the teachers identify areas of weakness in the children in their classes. They use this information to modify the curriculum. For example, in the area of language arts the teachers found that many children were deficient in concept development, verbal comprehension, and expression. In essence, these children lacked the necessary linguistic prerequisites for reading, that is, they did not have the background for a typical reading-readiness program. As a result, the teachers provide more concrete experiences for the children, actually involving them with objects and events, so they develop meanings on a first-hand basis. The teachers revised the reading-readiness curriculum to provide the necessary language foundation rather than assuming that the children had acquired this foundation prior to school enrollment.

The kindergarten teachers also play an active role in the process of specific remediation. They participate in weekly team staff meetings in which they share their observations of children as well as obtain information and hints for modifying classroom procedures to reinforce the work of the specialists. For example, if the speech and language specialist has found that a child has difficulty processing a three-stage direction, the teacher monitors the directions to that child in the classroom, first providing two-stage directions, then expanding the directions as the child demonstrates improvement in the resource room.

61

The teachers participate in the Shoe Box program. They help to identify children's needs, organize and select kits to meet these needs, and direct the peer-teaching program. In addition, throughout the day they meet with small groups of children and use a variety of materials and approaches which are adapted to each group's deficiencies.

Follow-up First-Grade Programs

The high-risk kindergarten children with language-learning problems identified in 1974-1975 were promoted to the same first-grade classroom. Therefore, 17 of the 28 children in this class have special needs.

The room was divided into four primary areas: pre-math, pre-reading, fine motor, and language. Each morning, between 9:30 and 11:30, small groups of children are rotated through these stations, as needed. Only two of the four stations operate during a given 20-minute interval. The stations are staffed by the learning disabilities specialist, the speech and language specialist, and a specialist in emotional handicaps. Children who do not participate in the small-group sessions receive individualized reading instruction from the classroom teacher, do seat work, or engage in special projects. The entire class participates in a 20-minute listening-skills program which is conducted by the speech and language specialist. Under this system, a given high-risk child receives from 40-100 minutes of specialized instruction each day.

The stations in the room have been numbered and color coded. At the inception of the program, each child was given a name tag on which his schedule was displayed according to the numbers and color codes. In a short time, the children independently moved from one station to another to meet their individual schedules. This organizational structure reduced the number of management problems while more effectively meeting the needs of each child.

IMPLICATIONS FOR THE FIRST-GRADE TEACHER

The first-grade teacher actively participated in the design of the program. She is the team leader; she maintains control of the curriculum and the rules of the room, and she participates in weekly staff meetings concerning specific children. She has ample opportunity to observe the children at the various stations and to gain an appreciation of the performance level of each child with respect to specific skills. She uses this information as she works with each child and the group, supplementing and reinforcing the work of the specialists.

MODEL CONTINGENCIES

The speech and language early intervention-prevention program at the Whitman School is a model for similar buildings with the following contingencies: (a) team teaching, (b) open-space classrooms, (c) a full-time speech and language specialist, and (d) readily available other special education support services.

Summary

The Mesa Public Schools prevention-early intervention program has mainstreamed educators rather than children. Specialists have been integrated into teaching teams and classroom teachers have been placed in the role of team coordinator with ultimate responsibility for each child's program. The close interactions with specialists have increased the teacher's sensitivity to individual differences and provided the necessary day-by-day support to meet childrens' needs. At the same time, the specialists have acquired a greater appreciation of curricular demands and learned to adapt their remedial programs to them.

Gouldsboro Grammar School
Gouldsboro, Maine

"Project Right to Achieve: An Individualized Kinder-garten-First Grade Program." has been in effect at the Gouldsboro Grammar School since September 1974. The project is partially supported by Title III funds. It required the development and implementation of a totally new curriculum with a substantial component devoted to the development of receptive and expressive verbal skills.

The School District

Gouldsboro Grammar School is one of 7 buildings (6 elementary schools and 1 high school) that constitute School Union #96. The district is located in a sparsely populated rural area of Down East Maine and serves 1,300 children. The elementary schools consist of kindergarten to eighth-grade classes. The residents of this middle- to low-income area earn their livelihood predominantly through canning, boat building, and lobster fishing.

Gouldsboro Grammar School serves 214 children. Prior to the inception of the individualized kindergarten-first-grade program, all classrooms were self-contained and traditional, in accord with the established pattern of the district.

The Gouldsboro Grammar School Program

"Right to Achieve" has replaced the kindergarten and first grade with a single, nongraded, individualized, 2-3 year primary program. It has a continuous curriculum that emphasizes language and cognitive skills. Three teachers (one with a background in special education), a full-time aide, a part-time aide, and student and adult volunteers implement the program. The project occupies a semi-open classroom which was created by removing part of the connecting wall between two adjacent rooms. Although the physical facility is open, the program is highly organized. About 44 children, half kindergartners and half first graders, are enrolled.

DEVELOPMENT OF THE PROGRAM

The staff organized and wrote progressive curricula in the areas of language, reading and writing, logical thinking, math, and physical education. They identified the principal concepts and skills which they hoped the children would achieve by the end of the usual first-grade year, and outlined a sequence of subskills necessary for the mastery of each major objective. The development of verbal skills was given high priority because many of the students come from relatively nonverbal homes, the distances between homes often preclude peer contacts, and few children attend nursery school.

None of the staff had had training or experience in the development of a language curriculum. Therefore, they called upon a member of the Communicative Disorders Department of the University of Maine to serve as a resource. With the assistance of the consultant, they developed specific objectives for receptive and expressive language (Pickering & Koelber, in press).

1. Given verbal directions, child will sort, according to class and function, pictures of familiar objects in his environment (e.g., fruits, vehicles, toys).
2. Given verbal directions, child will sort pictures of objects according to physical characteristics (e.g., shape, color, size).
3. Given verbal directions which use terms denoting position in space, child will perform appropriate actions (e.g., left, right, under, next to).
4. Given verbal directions commonly used in classroom instruction, child will perform appropriate actions (e.g., underline, color, draw a circle around).
5. Given pictures of familiar objects in his environment, child will name and describe items in terms

65

of class and function (e.g., banana, fruit, something to eat).

6. Given pictures of objects, child will name and describe items in terms of physical characteristics (e.g., ball, round, small).
7. In response to questioning, child will give basic information about himself (e.g., full name, address, age).
8. In response to questioning, child will say a word opposite in meaning to the one presented (e.g., hot/cold, up/down).
9. In response to questioning, child will use appropriate terms denoting time relations (e.g., seasons, months, yesterday, afternoon).
10. In response to questioning, child will label and describe feelings of self and others (e.g., sad, angry, scared).
11. Child will use basic grammatical structures accurately (e.g., pronouns, verb tenses, plurals).
12. Child will express himself, using affirmative, negative, and interrogative patterns where appropriate.
13. Child will use social idioms appropriately (e.g., hello, please, thanks).
14. Child will re-tell events of a story in correct sequence.
15. Child will relate past events in a connected narrative fashion.

Thematic units were developed to enable children to meet the language objectives. These units provide a content framework; they deal with topics such as school, self, family, community, and seasons. A series of activities, stratified according to level and complexity of verbal demands, was developed within each unit. Furthermore, the total curriculum is based on a spiral, that is, objectives are repeated in different contexts at varying levels of complexity. An example of a thematic unit follows (Pickering & Koelber, in press):

Thematic Unit: Winter

Specific Objectives to be worked on:
1. Child will define winter as a season
2. Child will sort and classify winter-related pictures
3. Child will state major weather aspects of winter (for example, cold, snow, sleet, ice).
4. Child will name at least five things people do only in winter (for example, wear warm clothes, put up storm windows, ride on snowmobiles, ice fish).
5. Child will name the four winter months (December— March).
6. Child will tell about at least two winter-related things he has done, in a narrative fashion.

Activities:

Sort pictures, sequence pictures (four seasons), create winter scene (draw or make collage), cut out from catalogue typical winter-day clothes, make snowman (real and/or from recycled packaging materials), try on sports apparel and equipment brought by teachers.

67

IMPLEMENTATION OF THE LANGUAGE PROGRAM

A language-screening battery is administered to prospective students during the spring preceding kindergarten enrollment. The battery consists of the Auditory Association subtest of the *Illinois Test of Psycholinguistic Abilities* (Kirk, McCarthy, & Kirk, 1975), and the Oral Commissions and Auditory Attention Span for Related Syllables subtests of the *Detroit Test of Learning Aptitude* (Baker & Leland, 1959). The staff uses the test data to make preliminary judgments on each child's linguistic abilities. At the beginning of the subsequent school year, the *Peabody Picture Vocabulary Test* (Dunn, 1965) is administered to all kindergarten children. On the basis of all data, the staff first tentatively places each child into one of two regular groups or a special needs group for language training. Each of these three large groups (comprising both kindergarten and first-grade children) is then divided into two smaller subgroups. The small size of each subgroup (5-8 children) facilitates pupil/teacher verbal interactions and allows for variations in activities as needed. At any time during the school year a child may be moved to a higher or lower group, based on the teacher's judgment of his or her performance.

During the first daily 30-minute activity period, the children attend their language groups. Each group simultaneously participates in the same thematic unit but at varying levels of abstraction and complexity. For example, while working on the theme of foods, children in the special needs groups handle, taste, and name common foods and identify their physical attributes. Instruction is necessarily highly structured and concrete. At the next level, children verbally describe a wider variety of foods, categorizing them according to the meals at which they might be eaten. Children in the higher groups work on a more abstract level, comparing, contrasting, and classifying foods in a number of different ways. A more sophisticated vocabulary is introduced, and the concepts developed in discussion are more complex (e.g., where foods come from).

Independent supplementary activities are devised for all six groups according to level of difficulty. They include drawing pictures of foods under appropriate headings (e.g., "breakfast," "lunch," and "dinner"), sorting picture cards into three or more categories, or printing lists of foods according to various classifications.

The children who would normally be classified as first graders remain in school the entire day; kindergartners are dismissed at noon. During the afternoon, the first graders are divided into three groups for additional language work based on the program "Developing Understanding of Self and Others" (Dinkmeyer, 1973). The children are encouraged to identify and talk freely about their feelings, goals, and behavior. They listen to stories containing problem situations and engage in open-ended discussions, which frequently are followed by role playing or puppet activities.

Role of the Consultant

The University of Maine consultant assisted in the development of objectives for the language curriculum. In addition, she observed the teachers during the language period and identified their difficulties in implementing the program. For example, at times, the consultant noted that teachers (a) were apt to pay more attention to more verbal children than to those who spoke little, (b) failed to provide adequate response time before presenting additional requests, (c) demonstrated a tendency to interrupt, and (d) overlooked the stratification of abstractness and complexity in verbal directions.

Based on these observations, the consultant conducted a skill-development program for the teachers. She facilitated enhancement of their abilities to communicate more effectively with the students. The open attitudes of the consultant and teachers permitted candid discussions of the observations which promoted changes in teacher behavior. On subsequent visits, the consultant has been able to reinforce these changes and to continue to provide constructive criticism regarding the language program.

69

Model Contingencies

The Gouldsboro Grammar School prevention-intervention program is a model for other buildings with the following contingencies: (a) an innovative leader who competently demonstrates the need for change to administrators; (b) competent, confident teachers who relate well to each other and are eager to improve their teaching skills; (c) a well-respected, school-oriented, child-centered consultant in speech and language; (d) a commitment to individual instruction; (e) open classrooms; (f) highly organized curriculum; and (g) aides and volunteers to supplement the work of the professional teaching staff.

Summary

The Gouldsboro prevention-intervention program is conducted entirely in the classroom. It exemplifies the coordination of public school and university personnel in the establishment of an individualized curriculum-based language program. It recognizes the importance of verbal language skills as the basis of reading, writing, and general academic achievement. It demonstrates how a relatively isolated school staff with no special services can coordinate available resources to meet the linguistic needs of children.

VI

Speech Deviations Programs

Seattle Public Schools
Seattle, Washington

The Seattle Public Schools are a large complex organization that serves about 62,000 children. The system consists of 85 elementary schools, 6 middle schools, 11 junior high schools and 12 high schools. Nearly 30% of the district's children are members of minority groups: 17% black, 2.3% Japanese, 2.6% Chinese, 2.1% Filipino, 1.4% Spanish, 1.6% American-Indian, and 2% other. School services, including those provided by speech-language pathologists, have been diversified to meet the children's needs.

Language, Speech, and Hearing Services

The Seattle schools have a well-developed, long-established language, speech, and hearing program. It provides a continuum of services that includes components for speech development, speech deviations, and communicative disorders. The program is accredited by the Professional Services Board of the American Speech and Hearing Association in recognition of its high-quality services.

Forty-one speech-language pathologists are on the school district staff. They use a variety of service and scheduling models based on the incidence and severity of problems among the children within each school. In some instances, speech-language pathologists are building based; in others, they provide itinerant services to 2-5 schools. Occasionally, a school with a large population of children with special needs has two building-based speech-language pathologists. The caseloads range from 13-65 children who are seen 1-5 times a week for 10-60 minutes. The needs of the children determine the nature and intensity of their programs.

The Speech Deviations Component

It is impossible to describe this program completely because of its size, the number of personnel involved, the range of the children's needs, and the scope of the staff's strengths. However, major characteristics of the speech deviations programs were identified through interviews with five classroom teachers, three speech-language pathologists, and the supervisor of the program. As a result, classroom teachers' typical practices with children who demonstrate speech deviations were identified.

BASIC PRINCIPLES

The speech deviations component is based on two principles: (a) children with speech deviations need to practice their newly acquired verbal skills in a variety of contexts, and (b) opportunities to practice these skills can be integrated into the routine of regular classrooms. The teachers support these principles. They emphasize clear verbal communication in all academic activities and facilitate the carry-over of new communicative skills from the semiprotective, clinically oriented speech class to the more natural classroom setting.

Children are screened for speech problems early in the school year. Once those with speech deviations are identified, the teachers stand ready to play an active role in the remedial programs outlined by the speech-language pathologist.

Through child-centered conferences with speech-language pathologists, teachers have become increasingly aware of specific sounds, deviant patterns in their production, and techniques for eliciting correct speech. Furthermore, they regard clear speech as basic to the language arts program. As one teacher commented, "I don't feel that correcting a child's speech deviation, when I know he can produce certain sounds clearly, is any different from correcting a child who says 'ain't'." Another said, "Speech and grammar have slid! I'm strict about them with all children. I don't do anything different with children who show speech deviations; I'm just more conscious of their needs."

TEACHER INVOLVEMENT

Speech-language pathologists and teachers have developed indirect and direct methods to use in the classroom to help children correct speech deviations. The classrooms I visited were self-contained. However, in each case individual instruction was implemented through daily conferences with the students. This system enables classroom teachers to work on speech incidentally during group activities, as well as to conduct direct speech-oriented tasks during individual conferences.

The teachers are aware of the immediate objectives for children with communicative deviations, and they continuously reinforce newly acquired speech patterns as they occur in any oral activity (e.g., reading, story telling, sharing time, or choral speaking). The teachers routinely provide a word of praise when warranted ("You're speaking so clearly!" or, "You remembered your '1' sounds!"). Also, during phonics games and activities, children with communicative deviations are grouped according to their speech needs so that attention is paid to the correct production of sounds as well as the recognition of sound-letter correspondence.

SPECIFIC TECHNIQUES

The speech-language pathologists use classroom materials, particularly books, during remedial sessions with the children. The teachers are apprised of the specific sounds that each child is able to read correctly so they can reinforce these behaviors in class. Also, the speech-language pathologists supply the children with new, short, high-interest books which the children share with their teachers and use to demonstrate newly acquired skills.

Mechanisms have been devised to remind the children to use their newly acquired speech patterns in the classroom. These carry-over techniques include blocks on which sounds have been printed, 3 X 5 cards containing phrases or sentences to be read to the teacher, and tally sheets on which children self-monitor their use of specific speech patterns. Such devices are kept on the children's desks to remind them and the teachers of the objectives. Also, teachers are given short lessons, lists of words to be practiced, and speech books to review with the children during individual conferences.

On occasion, the classroom teacher is involved directly in primary corrective measures. For example, one teacher was trained by the speech-language pathologist to assist a child in the production of the "k" and "g" sounds in isolation. The teacher follows specific procedures under the supervision of the speech-language pathologist. During the child's individual conference, the teacher helps him to achieve the appropriate tongue position which enables him to integrate the consonants with vowels. The speech-language pathologist provides the child with a small mirror so that during free moments he can continue to practice independently at his desk.

Model Contingencies

The Seattle Speech Deviations Program is a model for other districts with the following contingencies: (a) classroom teachers who are committed to oral communication as an essential component of the language arts programs; (b) recognition that newly acquired speech patterns should be practiced in a variety of contexts on a daily basis and are more efficiently established when responsibilities for this practice are shared; (c) speech-language pathologists who capitalize on opportunities to share techniques, materials, and concerns with interested classroom teachers; and (d) a speech and language supervisor who facilitates meeting children's individual needs through optional scheduling and service delivery systems.

Summary

The Seattle Public Schools' Speech, Language, and Hearing Program is comprehensive. The Speech Deviations Component includes direct and indirect involvement of classroom teachers, depending on children's needs. A primary strength of the program is the classroom teachers' willingness to share the responsibility of helping children to practice newly acquired speech patterns on a daily basis.

Amherst-Pelham Regional Schools   75
Amherst, Massachusetts

Located in the Connecticut River Valley, 27 miles north of Springfield, the Amherst-Pelham Regional School District serves a middle-income residential area with a population of 23,000, including resident students at the University of Massachusetts. The system consists of five elementary schools, a junior high school and a high school. The secondary buildings serve the towns of Leverett and Shutesbury in addition to Amherst and Pelham. About 4,000 students are enrolled in the district.

Speech and Language Services

The speech and language department provides a full range of services. The district maintains 4 full-time positions and one half-time position in speech pathology: 2 staff members are building based, one serves the secondary schools, one serves the three remaining schools, and the half-time member conducts a pre-school program. The speech-language pathologists work with 25-35 students, two or more times per week, depending on the type and severity of the problems. The program is accredited by the Professional Services Board of the American Speech and Hearing Association in recognition of its high-quality services.

The Speech Deviations Program

Classroom teachers are involved in the speech deviations program in three ways: (a) the speech-language pathologists regularly discuss their cases with the teachers through formal staffings and informal meetings, (b) the teachers observe their students in speech-language classes, and (c) the speech-language pathologists provide the teachers with two types of materials: those to be used with specific children and those to be used for general speech-language improvement activities.

THE BUILDINGS

The nature of the elementary school buildings contributes to the success of the program. Two of the schools consist only of open space classrooms. The others consist of self-contained classrooms that have been adjusted to accommodate traditional to modified open space arrangements. Furthermore, in most instances, classroom teachers have one or more assistants. The University of Massachusetts is located in Amherst and places many of its cadet teachers throughout the district. In addition, the open space classrooms are also staffed with full-time aides. The availability of these supportive personnel enable the teachers to conduct or direct specific speech-language-oriented activities for children in their rooms.

MATERIALS

The speech-language pathologists have organized an array of materials for use by classroom teachers. Although the nature and type of materials vary from one speech-language pathologist to another, each maintains a bountiful supply. In addition, the staff of speech-language pathologists prepared a series of general materials that are used to acquaint teachers with specific types of speechlanguage deviations and suggestions for their remediation. The general materials include information on auditory discrimination, auditory vocal association, lexical memory, vocal encoding, and auditory sequential memory. The materials briefly describe disabilities in these processes, offer general suggestions for remediation, and provide specific remedial activities that progress from "very easy" to "easy" to "hard."

In the case of auditory discrimination, for example, the material recognizes that children with such problems are likely to have difficulty in perceiving the similarities and differences among sounds. The teachers are advised to assist these children by initiating listening activities that involve grossly different sounds, then gradually moving to sounds in which the differences are more and more subtle. For example, "very easy" remedial activities include differentiating the high or low tones of a pitch pipe or, with the teacher standing outside of the children's range of vision, counting the number of times the teacher claps. "Easy" activities involve sorting pictures of objects, the names of which rhyme, or rhyming words to the name of a stimulus picture, or selecting a foil word from among four to six rhyming words that are read aloud by the teacher. "Hard" activities are composing nonsense rhymes or supplying a list of words that begin with the same sounds as a stimulus word. In addition, the materials suggest several individual and group games that may be used to strengthen children's listening skills.

The material on vocal encoding discusses the fact that some children have difficulty expressing ideas and concepts in spoken words. In these cases, the teachers first are asked to encourage the children to verbalize freely. The teachers are advised to stimulate conversation by selecting areas known to be of high interest to the children, to provide the children with attention and praise when they respond, and, as a first step, to reinforce the quantity rather than the quality of the children's spoken language. Suggested "easy" activities include asking the children to tell as many things about an object as they can (e.g., shape, color, function, major parts) or encouraging them to free associate in reponse to a given word. "Hard" activities are inventing story endings and defining words; "very hard" activities are discussing the meaning of proverbs or having a child teach a skill or concept to a classmate.

The specific materials distributed by the speech-language pathologists reflect their individual biases and philosophies. The materials range from original activities to commercially prepared worksheets, to individual plans of management that state behavioral objectives, exact techniques to be used, and criteria for measuring success. Regardless of their different styles, however, all the speech-language pathologists consistently supply teachers in their buildings with materials. The teachers use these materials according to their own pedagogical approaches, degree of interest in the programs, and available time.

Implications for Classroom Teachers

The involvement of classroom teachers in the speech deviations program varies, depending on the extent to which each feels the program is essential to the educational goals of the district. Despite the range of involvement, however, the classroom teachers as a group demonstrate an inordinate awareness of speech-language deviations. For example, one teacher reported that the speech-language pathologist had requested that she use a specific technique with a child for at least 3 minutes a day. She felt that it was impossible in a modified open space situation to carry out the practice privately but, she said, "His speech is always on my mind and I now can integrate his speech work everywhere—on the playground, in the lunchroom, in the classroom. The answers for some of these children always cannot be written materials."

On the other hand, some of the teachers who have been given specific programs of behavioral management have carried them out enthusiastically. They reported a sense of accomplishment in having contributed toward a measurable change in the speech behavior of their students. Furthermore, the general materials have motivated teachers to devise various types of activities and games which they use with groups of children with or without speech deviations. One teacher commented, "A lot of teachers don't realize that they already are doing speech work. They must be made aware that what they are doing is speech work. It feels good when a specialist is able to label what you are doing and point out a method to improve your effectiveness."

The speech-language pathologists use many techniques to promote carry-over of newly learned speech patterns into the classroom. These techniques include (a) workbooks that are kept in the children's desk or cubby holes for regular review by teachers, (b) weekly conferences with teachers regarding specific speech objectives, and (c) devices and props that are used to remind the children to use their corrected speech patterns. The speech-language pathologists also have organized and presented inservice programs for the teachers in which they discuss the identification of speech-language needs, general remedial approaches which may be adapted to individual children, and materials and techniques.

Program Contingencies

The speech deviations program in the Amherst-Pelham Regional Schools is a model for other districts with the following contingencies: (a) speech-language pathologists who regard the involvement of classroom teachers as essential to the success of the program; (b) speech-language pathologists who are willing to prepare materials according to the needs of classroom teachers; (c) classroom teachers who regard the improvement of oral skills as an integral component of the educational program; and (d) a coordinator of speech and language services who balances departmental unity with the individual, professional autonomy of staff members.

Summary

The speech deviations program in the Amherst-Pelham Regional Schools exemplifies the relation that can be established between speech-language pathologists and classroom teachers. It demonstrates the ability of speech-language pathologists to sensitize classroom teachers to the needs of children with speech deviations, provide them with materials and methods to assist in the remediation of these problems, and respect them for adapting information and materials to their individual pedagogical philosophies and practices. Classroom teachers are aware of speech deviations; they regard their remediation as essential and seek additional information and materials for children in their rooms. The central elements of the model are regular meetings between classroom teachers and speech-language pathologists, observations of speech classes by classroom teachers, and a variety of general and specific materials which speech-language pathologists share with classroom teachers.

VII

PROGRAMS FOR COMMUNICATIVE DISORDERS

Special School District of St. Louis County
Town and Country, Missouri

The Special School District of St. Louis County provides services in special education and vocational-technical training to 23 local school districts with a combined enrollment of 196,000 students. The area served by the special district surrounds the city of St. Louis but does not include it. The county is the twentieth wealthiest in the country.

The district's special education program is comprehensive. It includes 13 special schools, 130 special classrooms leased from local districts in the county, and itinerant programs for children with behavioral disorders, learning disabilities, speech and language deviations, hearing impairments, and other educational problems.

Speech and Hearing Services

The speech and hearing department provides a full range of services through its eight components: speech services to local schools, speech and language remediation to special schools, language development classes, speech development classes, hearing screening, clinical audiological assessments, hearing services to local schools, and classrooms for hearing-impaired children. The program is accredited by the Professional Services Board of the

American Speech and Hearing Association in recognition of its high-quality services.

LANGUAGE DEVELOPMENT CLASSES

The special district maintains 15 language development classes which are designed to meet the psycholinguistic and academic needs of children whose auditory-verbal skills are at least two years below age-level expectations. Eligibility for placement in these rooms is determined by the staff of a centralized diagnostic clinic maintained by the district. Six to 10 children are enrolled in each class according to their functional linguistic levels.

The language classes initially were instituted to provide two years of intensive remediation, after which the children were returned to regular classrooms. Currently, children may remain in the program longer, depending on their needs. The goal of the program is to enable the students to achieve at their expected academic grade levels.

The language classes are staffed by full-time teachers with training and background in communicative disorders and elementary education, and by teacher assistants who have had a minumum of two years of college. A speech-language pathologist also is assigned to each class to supplement the classroom teacher's speech and/or language program. This specialist may see children from the classes as often as eight times per week for small-group or individual remediation.

In addition, six itinerant language specialists are employed to serve the children after they have been mainstreamed. These specialists act as a liaison between the language rooms and regular classrooms; they maintain continuity in the remedial program and assist the regular teachers with any problems regarding the children placed in their rooms.

Mainstreaming

The process of returning a child to a regular classroom begins with a conference attended by the supervisor of language classes, a speech-language pathologist assigned full time to the language development rooms, and the principal of the accepting school. The principal designates a teacher who, he/she feels, will be able to continue effective management of the child. The team then discusses the child with the teacher, usually during the spring before placement. However, an open-entrance, open-exit policy permits children to be enrolled in the special language classes or mainstreamed out of them at any time during the school year. An essential aspect of inclusion in the mainstream is the regular teacher's willingnesss to accommodate to the needs of the child.

Once the placement is completed, the speech-language pathologist and special teacher jointly organize a support plan, including materials, for the accepting regular teacher. They discuss this plan and receive additional information for it from the itinerant language specialist to whom the mainstreamed child is assigned. The language specialist then works with the child on an individual basis 4-5 times a week for 30-60-minute periods and coordinates the remedial program with regular classroom demands. Simultaneously, the specialist works with the regular teacher to incorporate the support program into the child's daily academic activities. In time, interactions between the specialist and teacher are reduced in proportion to the child's accommodation to the regular curriculum.

Implications for Classroom Teachers

Children are placed in classrooms in which the teachers have indicated a willingness to adjust to individual special language-learning needs. The speech-language pathologist reviews the mainstreamed child's status with the teacher, using behaviorally oriented definitions of linguistic strengths and weaknesses. Depending on the needs, the teachers are sensitized to identify the children's abilities and difficulties in auditory reception, auditory association, verbal expression, auditory memory, grammar, sentence structure, auditory discrimination, reasoning and thinking skills, and vocabulary and linguistic sequencing. The teachers learn to apply remedial techniques to help the children to perform more adequately. For example, in the case of children with auditory sequencing problems, the teachers learn to segment their verbal directions and allow adequate time for the children to process one component at a time.

In addition to interactions with teachers, the speech and language staff has prepared a manual about language problems that includes remedial techniques for teachers to use in the classroom. For example, in the case of children with vocabulary difficulties, the manual suggests the following techniques:

1. GIVE A SYNONYM. Example: effect—outcome
2. USE THE WORD IN A SENTENCE WITH THE SYNONYM IN PARENTHESES. For example: What effect (outcome) will this red stain have on my mother's white sofa?
3. USE A NEGATIVE DEFINITION. Example: Cold—not hot
4. USE A GENERAL TERM TO GIVE A SPECIFIC MEANING. Example: a type of walk—trot
5. EXPLAIN VOCABULARY CONTEXT BY REWRITING AT A LOWER LEVEL. Example: A fortnight ago (two weeks ago), the papoose (young Indian child) ran away.
6. DRAMATIZE THE MEANING OF A CONCEPT. Use other children in the class or act out the word or situation yourself.
7. USE PICTURES OR ILLUSTRATIONS TO SHOW AS MANY MEANINGS AS POSSIBLE. This may seem concrete, but it is sometimes necessary. Stick figures work well.
8. GIVE SEVERAL DEFINITIONS FOR EACH NEW VOCABULARY WORD. fall—to go down; fall—a hairpiece
9. PUT VOCABULARY WORDS INTO A SENTENCE. Write at least one sentence for each mean-

ing. In this way the child can see how it is used in context. For example: (character) He's quite a character. Which character did you like best?

In short, the teachers' modifications in their own behavior provide compensatory methods of learning for children with language problems.

Model Contingencies

The communication disorders component of the special school district of St. Louis County is a model for other schools with the following contingencies: (a) self-contained classrooms for children with language problems; (b) itinerant speech-language pathologists, (c) classroom teachers who are willing to accept students from a special class, and (d) comprehensive special education support services.

Summary

The special district of St. Louis County operates classes for children whose verbal language skills are at least two years below chronological age-level expectations. The objective of the program is to mainstream the children as soon as possible. A speech and language clinician facilitates the mainstreaming process by serving as a liaison between the language development classroom and regular classroom, continuing to provide individual remedial instruction, and acting as a resource consultant to the regular classroom teacher.

Greensboro Public Schools
Greensboro, North Carolina

The Greensboro Public Schools Speech and Language program was completely reorganized in 1974. Previously, the speech clinicians divided their time equally among the

46 schools in the district with little consideration of the variance in number or severity of cases from building to building. In effect, they served schools rather than children.

The speech clinicians formed three committees to study this situation. One reviewed the literature on early language intervention; a second researched the incidence and grade levels of students in need of service; and the third reviewed alternative service and scheduling models. The committees' findings indicated a need for intensive speech and language services in the lower elementary grades. Subsequently, the clinicians proposed the establishment of a building-based service delivery model. The plan was approved and the program was restructured so that each clinician maintains responsibility for no more than two schools. The junior/senior high schools are served on demand and indirect services are provided to grades 4-6. This system has facilitated the development of a strong communicative disorders component in the lower elementary grades of the district.

The School System

Greensboro, a city with 160,000 residents and a school population of 28,000 is located in the industrial heart of North Carolina, the Piedmont triad. The school district's limits roughly parallel those of the city of Greensboro. The district supports 34 elementary schools, 8 junior high schools, and 4 high schools. The elementary schools are clustered and paired to assure racial balance (approximately one-third of the school population is black). As a result, some of the buildings consist entirely of lower elementary grades. The schools variously provide team teaching, open classrooms, and self-contained classrooms.

The Greensboro Public Schools maintain a comprehensive program for exceptional children which is committed to mainstreaming.

The Communicative Disorders Program

Speech-language pathologists are able to work intensively with children who demonstrate communicative disorders. Each pathologist serves one or two elementary schools and carries a caseload of 25-30 children who are seen individually or in small groups 15-30 minutes, 4-5 times per week. The speech-language pathologists regard themselves and are regarded by the teachers as bona fide members of the staffs of their schools. They attend faculty meetings and, in some instances, maintain a regular place on the agenda. They confer regularly with each classroom teacher in the building one or more times per week. It is a policy of the district for teachers to hold parent conferences following the first grading period of the year. The speech-language pathologists attend these conferences so that both the teachers and parents become aware of the children's speech and language goals and their relation to academic achievement.

87

The speech-language pathologists usually do not provide teachers with materials relative to language development. Instead, they encourage teachers to use remedial language techniques in all classroom activities. For example, the speech-language pathologists directly and indirectly train the teachers to provide alternative verbal choices, repeat (model) and expand the children's verbalizations, reinforce adequate verbal performances, establish realistic expectations, and use situations which seem important to the child to build language skills. The specialists discuss these techniques with the teachers, demonstrate their implementation in the classroom, and specifically relate them to stated objectives for each child.

Implications for Classroom Teachers

As a result of this program, classroom teachers have assumed greater responsibility for the development of specific speech and language skills. They recognize the relation between the development of verbal language and educational achievement. The speech-language pathologists have acquainted them with the critical elements of language development as described by Irwin and Marge (1972): auditory skills, perceptual skills, concept formation, oral language training, and syntax. The teachers have become more aware of the relation between the linguistic components of language (phonology, semantics, and syntax) and the conceptual system that underlies verbal behavior. They continuously reinforce linguistic skills and directly participate in the individual remedial programs outlined by the speech-language pathologist. For example, in the case of children whose inability to name shapes seems related to perceptual-conceptual problems, the classroom teachers assist in establishing the concepts for shapes prior to demanding the use of their names. On the other hand, when children demonstrate syntax disturbances, the teachers model and expand the children's utterances, reinforcing changes as they occur.

88

Model Contingencies

The communicative disorders component of the speech and language program in the Greensboro Public Schools is a model for similar situations with the following contingencies: (a) entire elementary schools consist of lower elementary classes; (b) a speech and language specialist is assigned to each school on a full- or half-time basis; (c) the administration and classroom teachers acknowledge the relation between the development of auditory-verbal skills and reading and writing; (d) speech-language pathologists ascribe to the belief that their services are an integral part of the educational process, some aspects of which may be implemented effectively by classroom teachers.

Summary

The Greensboro Public Schools' communicative disorders program has established speech-language pathologists as bona fide members of lower elementary school faculties. It has instituted a mechanism for daily interactions between teachers and speech clinicians. The communicative disorders program is an integral aspect of the total educational process, philosophically and pragmatically. Speech-language pathologists share techniques with classroom teachers who assume a major responsibility in fulfilling the program's goals.

REFERENCES

Arlt, A. B., & Goodban, M. T. A comparative study of articulation acquisition based on a study of 240 normals, aged three to six. *Language, Speech and Hearing Services in Schools*, 1976, **7**, 173-180.

Baker, H. H., & Leland, B. *Detroit Tests of Learning Aptitude.* Indianapolis: Bobbs-Merrill, 1959.

Boehm, A. E. *Boehm Test of Basic Concepts.* New York: Psychological Corporation, 1971.

Carroll, J. B. Words, meanings and concepts. *Harvard Educational Review,* 1964, **34**, 178-202.

Carrow, E. Assessment of speech and language in children. In J. E. McClean, D. E. Yoder, & R. L. Schiefelbusch (Eds.), *Language intervention with the retarded: Developing strategies.* Baltimore: University Park Press, 1972.

Chappell, G. E. A cognitive-linguistic intervention program: Basic concept formation level. *Language, Speech and Hearing Services in Schools*, 1977, **8**, 23-32.

Clark, E. C. Some aspects of the conceptual basis for first language acquisition. In R. L. Schiefelbusch & L. L. Lloyd (Eds.), *Language perspectives–acquisition, retardation and intervention.* Baltimore: University Park Press, 1974.

Cooper, F. S. How is language conveyed by speech? In J. J. Kavanaugh & I. G. Mattingly (Eds.), *Language by ear and by eye.* Cambridge, Mass.: MIT Press, 1972.

Dinkmeyer, D. *Developing understanding of self and others.* Circle Pines, Minn.: American Guidance Service, 1973.

Dunn, L. M. *Peabody Picture Vocabulary Test.* Circle Pines, Minn.: American Guidance Service, 1965.

Frankenburg, W. K., & Dodds, J. B. *The Denver Developmental Screening Test.* Denver: University of Colorado Press, 1968.

Freeman, G. G. The assessment of oral language as a precursor of reading. In W. Otto, C. W. Peters, & N. Peters (Eds.), *Reading problems: A multidisciplinary perspective.* Reading, Mass.: Addison-Wesley, 1977.

Healey, W. C. *Standards and guidelines for comprehensive language, speech and hearing programs in the schools.* Washington, D. C. : American Speech and Hearing Association, 1974.

91

Irwin, J., & Marge, M. *Childhood language disabilities*. New York: Appleton-Century-Crofts, 1972.

Kavanaugh, J. F. (Ed.). *Communicating by language: The reading process*. (Proceedings of the Conference on Communicating by Language: The Reading Process, New Orleans, La., Feb. 11-13, 1968, convened by NICHHD.) Washington, D. C.: Government Printing Office, 1968.

Kirk, S. A., McCarthy, J. J., & Kirk, W. D. *Illinois Test of Psycholinguistic Abilities* (rev. ed.). Urbana, Ill.: University of Illinois Press, 1975.

Knight, N. F. Structuring remediation in a self-contained classroom. *Language, Speech and Hearing Services in Schools*, 1974, **5**, 198-203.

Lee, L. L., Koenigsknecht, R. A., & Mulhern, S. T. *Interactive language development teaching*. Evanston, Ill.: Northwestern University Press, 1975.

Mardell, C. D., & Goldenberg, D. S. *Developmental Indicators for the Assessment of Learning*. Highland Park, Ill.: Dial, 1975.

Pickering, M., & Koelber, P. The speech pathologist and the classroom teacher: A team approach to language development. *Language, Speech and Hearing Services in Schools* (in press).

Report of the Legislative Council, American Speech and Hearing Association. *Asha*, 1977, **19,** 138.

Richardson, S. O. Language training for mentally handicapped children. In R. L. Schiefelbusch, R. H. Copeland, & J. O. Smith (Eds.), *Language and mental retardation*. New York: Holt, Rinehart, & Winston, 1967.

Robertson, M. L., & Freeman, G. G. Applying diagnostic information to decisions about placement and treatment. *Language, Speech and Hearing Services in Schools*, 1974, **5**, 187-193.

Stephenson, W. T. The Oakland Schools prevention plan. *Language, Speech and Hearing Services in Schools*, 1974, **5**, 55-58.

Templin, M. *Certain language skills in children, their development and interrelationships* (Institute of Child Welfare Monograph, Series 26). Minneapolis: University of Minnesota Press, 1957.

Venezky, R. L. Spelling-to-sound correspondence. In J. F. Kavanaugh (Ed.), *Communicating by language: The reading process*. Washington, D.C.: Government Printing Office, 1968.

Yoder, D. E. Personal communication, February 7, 1974.

Zemmol,C. S. A priority system of case-load selection. *Language, Speech and Hearing Services in Schools*, 1977, **2**, 85-98.

APPENDIX

Representative Speech and Language Tests

Phonological Decoding.

Goldman-Fristoe-Woodcock Test of Auditory Discrimination:

Selection of a series of stimulus pictures from among three foils, the names of which vary by one phoneme. Recorded stimuli are presented in noisy and quiet backgrounds.

Templin Short Test of Sound Discrimination:

Differentiation of paired nonsense-syllable stimuli, some of which are the same, others of which vary by one phoneme.

Wepman Auditory Discrimination Test:

Differentiation of paired word stimuli, some of which are the same, others of which vary by one phoneme.

Phonological Encoding.

Fisher-Logemann Test of Articulation Competence.

Goldman-Fristoe Test of Articulation.

McDonald Deep Test of Articulation.

Templin-Darley Tests of Articulation.

Naming a series of pictures of objects and actions, the labels for which systematically contain phonemes and phonemic combinations.

Decoding Semantics.

Peabody Picture Vocabulary Test:

Selection of pictures of stimulus words from among three foils.

Encoding Semantics.

Michigan Picture Vocabulary Test (Subtest of the Michigan Picture Language Inventory):

Naming stimulus pictures displayed with two foils when the sets of three have conceptual relations.

Decoding Syntax.

Assessment of Children's Language Comprehension (ACLC):

Selection of pictures that depict increasingly long sequences of syntactic elements.

Northwestern Syntax Screening Test:
  Selection of pictures that depict a variety of syntactic forms.
Test for Auditory Comprehension of Language (TACL):
  Selection of pictures that depict various language structures.

Encoding Syntax.

Carrow Elicited Language Inventory:
  Repetition of statements consisting of various language structures.
Northwestern Syntax Screening Test:
  Repetition of picture descriptions consisting of various syntactic forms.

Language Batteries.

Detroit Tests of Learning Aptitude (Language Subtests).
Illinois Test of Psycholinguistic Abilities.
Utah Test of Language Development.
  Series of subtests designed to measure various linguistic components.

96

Publications
of the
Leadership Training Institute/Special Education and
the National Support Systems Project
University of Minnesota

Distributors

Audio Visual Library Services   For information on single copy
University of Minnesota   price and quantity order dis-
3300 University Ave.   counts, write to address given.
Minneapolis, MN 55414

Davis, J. (Ed.). *Our forgotten children: Hard-of-hearing pupils in the regular classroom.* (1977)
Spicker, H. H., Anastasiow, N. J., & Hodges, W. L. (Eds.). *Children with special needs: Early development and education.*
Reynolds, M. C. (Ed.). *Psychology in the schools: Proceedings of the conference on psychology and the process of schooling in the next decade.* (1971)
Reynolds, M. C., & Davis, M. D. (Eds.). *Exceptional children in regular classrooms.* (1971)

Council for Exceptional Children For information on single copy
Publication Sales   price and quantity order dis-
1920 Association Ave.   counts, write to address given.
Reston, VA 22091

Martin, G. J., & Hoben, M.   *Supporting visually impaired students in the mainstream.* (1977)
Deno, S. L., & Mirkin, P. K. *Data-based program modification: A manual.* (1977)
Birch, J. W. *Hearing impaired pupils in the mainstream.* (1976)
Birch, J. W. *Mainstreaming: Educable mentally retarded children in regular classes.* (1974)
Deno, E. N. (Ed.). *Instructional alternatives for exceptional children.* (1972)
Hively, W., & Reynolds, M. C. (Eds.). *Domain-referenced testing in special education.* (1975)
Jones, R. A. (Ed.). *Mainstreaming: The minority child in regular classes.* (1976)
Parker, C. A. (Ed.). *Psychological consultation: Helping teachers meet special needs.* (1975)
Reynolds, M. C. (Ed.). *Mainstreaming: Origins and implications.* (1976)
Thiagarajan, S., Semmel, D. S., & Semmel, M. I. *Instructional development for training teachers of exceptional children: A sourcebook.* (1974)
Weinberg, R. A., & Wood, F. H. (Eds.). *Observation of pupils and teachers in mainstreaming and special education settings: Alternative strategies.* (1975)

Leadership Training Institute/Special Education
253 Burton Hall   For information, write to
178 Pillsbury S. E.   address given.
University of Minnesota
Minneapolis, MN 55455

Reynolds, M. C. (Ed.). *National technical assistance systems in special education: Report of the conference in Washington, D. C.* (1976)

Reynolds, M. C. (Ed.). *Special education and school system decentralization.* (1975)

MISCELLANEOUS

Peterson, R. L. "Mainstreaming: A working bibliography." (A mimeographed, periodically revised bibliography of books and articles relating to "mainstreaming.")

Peterson, R. L. "Mainstreaming training systems, materials, and resources: A working list." (A mimeographed, periodically revised listing of training systems and other "mainstreaming" resources.)

IN PREPARATION

Deno, E. N. *Mainstreaming: Learning disabled, emotionally disturbed, and socially maladjusted children in regular classes.* (Winter 1977)

Lundholm, K., & Prouty, R. W. *Change in the schools: A casebook.* (Winter 1977)

98

National Support Systems Project
253 Burton Hall   For information, write to ad-
178 Pillsbury S.E.   dress given.
University of Minnesota
Minneapolis, MN 55455

IN PREPARATION

Reynolds, M. C. (Ed.). *Futures of education.* (Winter 1977)

Grosenick, J. K., & Reynolds, M. C. (Eds.). *Teacher education: Renegotiating roles for mainstreaming.*